© Alex Williams

About the Author

Brandy Williams is a Witch and a Pagan Magician who loves the magic of making. She weaves protection and caring into every hat she knits for her friends. She enjoys experimenting with natural dyes from plants she grows in her garden. She also loves applying her extensive knowledge of magical correspondences and techniques to the physical charms she makes. You can connect with her at www.brandywilliamsauthor.com.

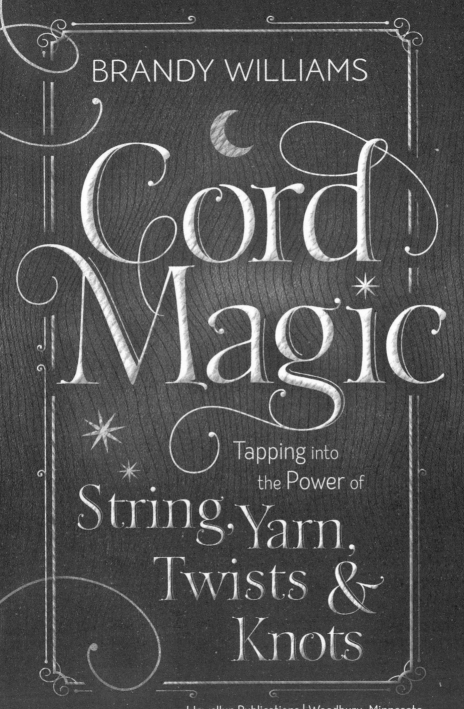

BRANDY WILLIAMS

Cord Magic

Tapping into
the Power of

String, Yarn,
Twists &
Knots

Llewellyn Publications | Woodbury, Minnesota

FIRST EDITION
Third Printing, 2022

Book design by Samantha Peterson
Cover design by Shannon McKuhen
Editing by Laura Kurtz
Illustrations by Wen Hsu
Illustrations on pages 77 and 245 by Llewellyn Art Department

Llewellyn Publications is a registered trademark of Llewellyn Worldwide Ltd.

Library of Congress Cataloging-in-Publication Data
Names: Williams, Brandy, author.
Title: Cord magic : tapping into the power of string, yarn, twists & knots
Description: First edition. | Woodbury, Minnesota : Llewellyn Publications,
    2021. | Includes bibliographical references and index. | Summary: "About
    cord magic and knot magic; includes making a cord, numerology (of knots,
    threads, etc.), color symbolism, various fabrics, weaving/cord goddesses
    of different cultures, special projects, etc"— Provided by publisher.
Identifiers: LCCN 2020057835 (print) | LCCN 2020057836 (ebook) | ISBN
    9780738766058 (paperback) | ISBN 9780738766782 (ebook)
Subjects: LCSH: Magic. | Ritual. | Cordage—Religious aspects. | Knots and
    splices—Religious aspects.
Classification: LCC BF1623.C66 W66 2021 (print) | LCC BF1623.C66 (ebook)
    | DDC 133.4/3--dc23
LC record available at https://lccn.loc.gov/2020057835
LC ebook record available at https://lccn.loc.gov/2020057836

Llewellyn Worldwide Ltd. does not participate in, endorse, or have any authority or responsibility concerning private business transactions between our authors and the public.

All mail addressed to the author is forwarded but the publisher cannot, unless specifically instructed by the author, give out an address or phone number.

Any internet references contained in this work are current at publication time, but the publisher cannot guarantee that a specific location will continue to be maintained. Please refer to the publisher's website for links to authors' websites and other sources.

Llewellyn Publications
A Division of Llewellyn Worldwide Ltd.
2143 Wooddale Drive
Woodbury, MN 55125-2989
www.llewellyn.com
Printed in the United States of America

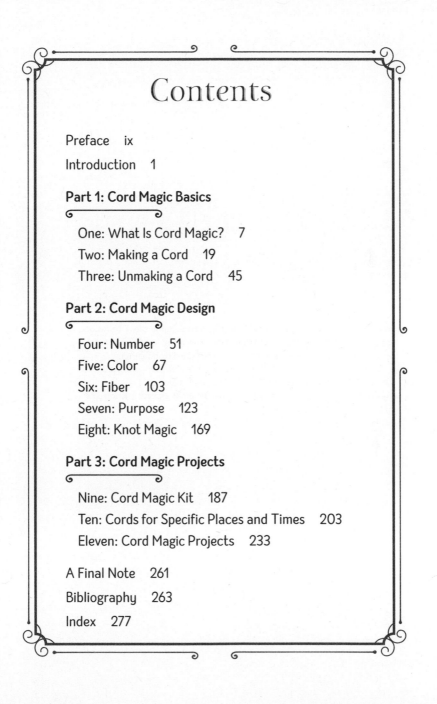

Contents

Preface

I learned how to twist cord from Rhea Loader. She knows the simple method used to make rope and taught a group of my friends together. For years, we all held classes and workshops showing other people the technique. We made cords for every possible magical purpose and wore them to every Pagan party.

That was just the start of our teaching careers; many of us went on to accept apprentices and lead magical groups. After a decade of teaching a beginner's class, I was ready to dive into more in-depth work. I wrote *Practical Magic for Beginners* to capture the material I give people just starting on their adventures in magic. When newcomers asked me to teach them, I could hand them the book!

Since then, I've been heads-down in creating new ways of thinking about the magics that we do. I've made space for women and other not-male genders in Ceremonial Magic, which was largely built by and for men. I've connected our current practice to the Pagan teachers of the past who built philosophical and religious frameworks as sophisticated and life-affirming as any of the major religions on the planet. I've linked up with other people working on these ideas too, and we write together and talk on podcasts and teach at conferences.

Practical magic never goes out of fashion. However lofty our spiritual goals, as long as we are physical beings we'll need to have a place to stay and food to eat, good health, and companionship and love. Magic helps us to get and keep those things. I've continued to do the candle spells of practical magic and the cord spells my young friends and I created together.

One day I was packaging a birthday present for a friend. It had a nice notebook and a fancy pen for jotting down ideas. It needed something else though. I grabbed some embroidery floss from my collection and picked green for health, yellow for happiness, and red for protection. The coven was gathering to meet that night so I had a houseful of people. I grabbed one of my coven mates and asked him to help me twist the cord. It was the first time he'd seen the technique and he instantly fell in love with it. "Hey," he said, "you could write about this!"

That was how I came to write this book. It brought me back to the fun I had making cords with my friends. One summer, three of my friends and I drove to California to attend a Pagan conference. We drove all day and night into the next day. We didn't stop until we reached the ocean. We tumbled out of the car, happy to stretch our legs. "Hey," I said, "let's make a cord to remember this." We each picked a color: blue-green for the ocean, beige for the sand, light blue for the sky, and yellow for our happiness. We made it together and cut it into sections for each of us to carry away.

Later at the conference, I taught a cord magic workshop. Sitting on a grassy field, I talked about the building blocks of magic, color, and number and simple affirmations. Then I broke out the bags of yarn and tossed them to the crowd. The field exploded with color as people measured out lengths and twisted them together, laughing and making magic with each other.

I hope cord magic brings you happy fun as well.

Introduction

My cell phone buzzed. Why would Pat be calling me at this time of night? When I picked it up, Pat said frantically, "Cathy is missing!"

Cathy was a sweet teenager, shy and trusting, and her mother tended to hover over her, so I didn't panic immediately. "Tell me what happened. Where did she go?"

"She left her friend's house two hours ago. She was supposed to come straight back."

I felt a jolt of alarm, but I kept my voice calm. "Does she have her cell phone?"

"No, she left it at home. I've called everywhere. I'm so worried," Pat said. "Please help her get home to me."

I walked into the bedroom. "What's your favorite color?" I asked.

"Blue," she said without hesitation.

With one hand I sorted through my basket of embroidery floss. "What's Cathy's favorite color?"

"Pink."

"Got it," I said. I picked a light yellow thread for my optimism that she would quickly be safe at home. "Now imagine a cord between yourself and Cathy."

"It's always there," she said.

"Hang on to it," I said. "Imagine yourself tugging gently on the cord. You're going to keep pulling gently until she comes home." That gave her something to do besides worry. "Call me in an hour or sooner if you have an update. I'll do a working for her."

Even by yourself, it only takes a minute or two to twist a cord. As I twisted the yarn I visualized Cathy home safe, Pat relieved and happy, and the two of them bound together by the cord. When it was finished, I tied a loose knot in the cord and said "Come home safe!"

Most of the time when we do a spell or magical working, we have time to shop for materials, assemble the tools, and carefully shape the magical intention into a clear sentence. When an emergency strikes though, the magic needs to be instant and decisive.

A cord is a talisman created for a specific purpose using fiber thread. The material of the cord can be cotton, wool, leather, or a synthetic substance such as nylon. As a physical object, it carries the energies of fiber and dye color and can incorporate other objects such as beads of stone and wood. As a talisman, it leverages associations we make with numbers, colors, and the cycles of time.

Magic means making things happen when you need them to happen. First you need to know what you want to accomplish and then figure out a way to state that clearly. Your goals might be to get a house, find a job, recover from an injury, heal a friendship. Magic leverages knowledge to manifest that goal using our personal associations and the common meanings of the materials used in our spells and rites. Finally, magic sends the intention out into the world.

Cord magic is one of the easiest and most satisfying ways to make magic. Cords are flexible. You can make them as standalone talismans or use them to add power to other talismans. Because they are so easy and inexpensive to make, they encourage creativity. You can experiment with textures, colors, and sizes. You can take the projects straight out of this book or use them to spark your own ideas.

Cords are discreet. Everyone uses string! Crafters make cords to use in jewelry. You can make cords in public and wear them in everyday life and no one will be the wiser. Cords are easy to incorporate into clothing or to hide in a pocket or bag. They're the ultimate portable tool.

This book covers the tools, techniques, and knowledge you need to make cords. You can read the book straight through or jump to the section that you need right now. The worksheets explore your own meanings for color, number, and fiber. When you fill them out, you will have your own references. If you need to get started right away, the quick references list common magical meanings. You can scan through the "Purpose" chapter to customize the intention that fits your needs, or you can turn to the "Cord Magic Projects" section and make one of the cords described there.

> **Tip:** Photocopy the worksheets to make your own workbook so you can quickly reference your own meanings to put together your cords.

What happened to Cathy? Almost an hour later, Pat called back. "She's home," she said with great relief. "She said she suddenly felt like she was in trouble with me. She's sorry she took so much time to get home." I breathed a sigh of relief and untied the knot in the cord, a wish fulfilled.

When I saw Pat and Cathy the next week, I gave Cathy the cord. "You can wear this or keep it in your pocket or purse," I said. "It's a talisman to keep you safe." I gave Pat a piece of the cord. "You can use this to help feel your connection with her."

Not every story is as dramatic as Cathy's (thank goodness!), but it demonstrates how versatile cords can be. String is magical because it makes something useful from amazingly simple materials. The very act of creating string brings separate things together. Add color and a mesmerizing twist and the cord makes magic itself visible and tangible. Making a cord plucks magic from the air.

Part 1
Cord Magic Basics

Cords are one of the easiest and most creative ways to create magical talismans. The chapters in this section explore some of the ways people have used cords throughout history and around the world. The next step is to make a cord. It takes much longer to explain how to do it than to actually do it! Once you get the hang of it, you can make a cord in just a few minutes. Of course, it's important to know how to manage any magic we do, so we'll look at unmaking a cord too.

This book contains worksheets you can fill out with your own personal references. It also contains quick references with standard or sample meanings. An exercise is an action you practice to learn to make cords. A charm gives specific instructions that result in a completed cord. To "charm" means to chant over an object or speak an incantation, and the object itself is a charm, also called an amulet or talisman. When you create a cord, you are performing the magical action of charming to make a charm.

one
What Is Cord Magic?

You probably already do cord magic. Have you ever given a friendship bracelet to someone? Maybe you went to a ritual and someone wrapped a string around your wrist. It's such a universal magic that almost every culture around the world and throughout history has some form of magical cord.

Cord Magic is Ancient

Making a thread, dyeing it, and tying it around ourselves is one of the most ancient magics we know.

How old is cord magic?

A sailor looks up at the linen cloth hanging flat in the rigging. Still no wind. Three days becalmed and the rations are running low. He pulls out a thin rope tied with elaborate knots. Well, there's nothing else to do, he needs help now. Blowing on the rope to get the process started, he solemnly unties the knot. "Blow, wind, blow!" he says, an invocation and a prayer.

Older than that.

A dark-haired woman sits cross-legged with a bowl in her lap. The women sitting around the fire pit look up at her expectantly. Taking the roving in one hand, she begins to twirl the spindle, drawing out the wool to form a thin thread. As she spins, she softly hums a blessing for warmth and health.

Even older than that!

The dry stalks rattle in the late summer heat. A Neanderthal woman crushes the flax stalks between her hands to pick out the fibers. She rubs the fibers between her hands to combine them, adding more stalks as the string takes shape. She'll need an extra strong thread to take the weight of the holed stone she found. Wearing holed stones always brings luck. She's so absorbed in her work it takes her a while to notice the human woman quietly watching her work. The human woman offers a handful of flax stalks she's gathered. Huh. Turns out humans are teachable.

The human woman works hard and laughs easily. A tedious task goes more quickly with company. The Neanderthal takes off her necklace and slides off the shell she had been wearing. On an impulse, she hands it to the human woman. Eyes wide, the human puts the shell on her string and ties it around her neck, then puts her hands together and bows her head in thanks. Turns out humans can learn about magic too.

The oldest string is 90,000 years old. It was found in a cave in France which Neanderthals used long before our own human ancestors made it to Europe.[1] Adding this together with similar discoveries, scientists today are leaning toward the idea that early humans learned tool and string making from our evolutionary kissing cousins. Neanderthals used string to wear shells and the occasional holed animal tooth. Maybe it was just for decoration, but it's a lot of trouble to take for a decoration! Even today, people wear shells, teeth, and stones for magical protection.

We can see that string has been used for jewelry but can't know for sure that the pendants were magical. We do know that when the historical record opens, the magic of stone and string was already ancient.

Kasap leans against the wall, waiting for his turn at court. As he waits, he surreptitiously fingers the edge of his cloak. Hopefully, if anyone sees him, they'll think he's just fidgeting. Actually he's rubbing the stone bead he's knotted into the fringe. The stone is the one that brings favor from rulers, surely it will help in court. The knot holds his whispered wish to win the suit. Maybe he can finally get Iddin to return that loan!

Kasap might have read the Neo-Babylonian *Book of Stones* which lists the magical properties of specific minerals.[2] He and his

---

1. Barras, "World's oldest string found at French Neanderthal site."

2. Reiner, *Astral Magic in Babylonia*, 121–128.

friends wore stone beads to protect them from disease, enemies, and the anger of the gods.

Gemstone magic is well understood. But it isn't just the pendant that offers protection, the cord itself carries power. One of the Egyptian hieroglyphs for a magical pendant, *SA*, is a pictogram of a loop of rope.[3] *Himala*, the Arabic word for "amulet," refers to a cord worn around the neck as well as the amulet hung on the cord.[4]

What makes the cord itself magical? Partly it's the material. Flax makes a comfortable and lightweight fabric, which would be especially welcome if your only alternatives are leather and fur.

It's also partly the color. Dyeing a cord enhances its power. Kasap and his friends wore their magical stones by stringing them on red, black, or white cords.[5] Witches today still make cords of red, black, and white. So if someone asks you why, tell them the idea is at least as old as the Babylonians.

It's easy to understand why the colors black and white show up in cords. Sheep give wool in those colors, along with brown and gray. There aren't any red sheep, though—to get that color, you have to dye the fabric. It turns out we've been doing that for quite a long time too.

Red, black, and white aren't the only colors humans have been using in threads. Scientists found flax thread that is 30,000 years old in a Russian cave, and the thread was dyed turquoise.[6] The archaeologists found plant roots that could have been used for dyeing along with the thread in the cave. The color range was reported to include

---

3. Pinch, *Magic in Ancient Egypt*, 108.

4. Budge, *Amulets and Superstitions*, 13.

5. Reiner, *Astral Magic*, 125.

6. Kvavadze et al., "30,000 Years old wild flax fibers."

yellow, red, blue, violet, black, brown, green, and khaki. You could make a rainbow pride flag with those colors!

Cord Magic is Spiritual

There is something about string that lends itself to remembering our spiritual nature. Maybe it's the fact that we use thread to tie things together. Maybe it's the primal connection of cord with life. Before we were born, we were linked with our mothers through an umbilical cord that literally kept us alive until we were ready to emerge into the world and breathe and eat on our own. Whatever the reason, cord magic is a custom that Jewish, Hindu, Buddhist, Christian, Shinto, and Pagan traditions hold in common. Here are some examples.

The simplest form of cord magic is a single colored string worn for protection and good luck. One famous string is the red Kabbalah cord. Usually these are pieces of a length of yarn that has been wound around Rachel's tomb. The Jewish matriarch was the mother of Joseph and Benjamin and was herself known for being generous and kind. Her blessing on the cord protects whomever wears it from malice and misfortune.[7] Celebrities such as Madonna made the "Kabbalah string" famous.[8] Today, you can buy a piece of a string that has been wound around Rachel's tomb from many sources online.

The red string may be tied around a baby's wrist. One possible source of this custom is the story in Genesis 38.[9] The story goes that Judah's wife, Tamar, was giving birth to twin boys. It was important to know which was born first as he would be Judah's

---

7. Teman, "The Red String."

8. The Kabbalah Center, "The Red String."

9. Rabbi Ullman, "The Red String."

heir. As Tamar's labor went on, one of the infants stuck his hand out of the womb. The midwife wrapped a cord around his wrist and said, "This one was born first!" Then the boy pulled his hand back. Finally a baby emerged into the arms of the midwife … but he was not wearing the red thread! He was the second twin. He ended up being recognized as the first born and the heir, while the baby with the red thread emerged after him and was forever the second child.

Red thread also features in Christian customs. Some families pass on a thread ritual as a tradition.[10] The mother or grandmother of a newborn baby wraps a red thread around the tiny wrist. This custom links the family to the Christian tradition and offers a blessing to the newborn child.

String can also be braided into plaits, twisted into rope, and woven into fabric, and each of these actions has magical power. Jewish people wear prayer shawls called *tallit* that may be tied with blue fringes called *Tzizith*.[11] They may also have a border in blue. This comes from a divine instruction in Numbers 15:38: "Throughout the generations to come you are to make tassels on the corners of your garments, with a blue cord on each tassel." The color blue reminds the wearer of the sky and of the ocean, which are reflections of the divine presence. The Tzizith calls the mind of the wearer to remember to pray.[12]

Pennsylvania Dutch women use red wool in healing. The thread is passed over the body of the sick person and then hung

---

10. Mowry, "The Story Behind Our Bracelets."

11. Lockshin, "What Do Tzitzit Represent?"

12. Kluge, *The Tallit*, 13.

in fireplace smoke. The scarlet thread symbolizes Christ's sacrifice and carries his power of healing.[13]

Christians create crafts from yarn, such as shawls, blankets, and caps. Groups of people pray over them to provide a blessing for the people receiving them. The woven goods are given to families with newborns to protect the children, to sick people at home or in hospitals, and to people and families who have lost loved ones. These lovely gifts bring the message of care and a hope for healing and comfort.[14]

It's important to acknowledge that while we may recognize these as forms of cord magic, Christian and Jewish families may prefer not to think of these as magical actions but instead as carrying the blessings of God for the recipients.

Other religions connect thread with divine power. Visitors to Hindu temples sometimes receive a thread called a *kalava*.[15] The commercial skeins of this yarn generally combine red and gold threads. When my partner, Alex, and I traveled to Varanasi, we visited the great temple of Shiva, Kashi Vishwanath. A priest performed a puja for us. After he spoke prayers for us in Sanskrit, he had us cross our hands and wrapped a kalava around each of our wrists, Alex's right wrist and my left wrist, a ritual meant to capture the blessing of Shiva. The priest specifically gave us the blessing as a married couple together.

At a Buddhist monastery in Sri Lanka, the monks wind a spool of white thread while they chant Buddhist verses. Afterward, they give pieces of the thread for free to anyone who visits and asks for

---

13. Donmoyer, *Powwowing in Pennsylvania*, 118.

14. Jorgensen, *Knitting into the Mystery*, 11–13.

15. Bhatnagar, *My Hindu Faith and Periscope*, 61.

them so the wearer can be reminded of the power of the Buddha's words. They call this string a *pirit nul* or blessed thread.[16]

Buddhist monks in Thailand bless a white string called *sai sin*. Visitors to temples might have one tied around their wrist. This string is also used to decorate the temples at festival times. During wedding ceremonies, guests may tie white string around the wrists of the couple to give them blessings. The thread is also used in memorial ceremonies, where the string is wound around the crematorium to wish the deceased blessings in their next lives.[17]

Thread can be used to transmit power. A Buddhist ritual places divine power in a vase of water that is later used as an offering. The ritualist holds one end of the thread to their heart and ties the other end to the vase. Mantras are then spoken that consecrate the water in the vase.[18]

Many years ago, the Gaden Shartse monks visited Seattle on one of their cultural tours to give a concert. While in town, they stopped in a local Buddhist temple and gave a public White Tara empowerment that I was lucky enough to attend. The empowerment involves learning to chant a mantra and make a visualization of the goddess. During the ceremony the monks tied thread, in this case brown, around all our wrists. I still have my thread! Since White Tara bestows health and long life, I wear it when my health is threatened. I also wear it when I chant for friends who are facing life-threatening illnesses.

I have a statue of White Tara that has a white thread tied around her wrist. The statue is hollow, and prayers and mantras are written on paper and inserted in the statue while the monks

---

16. Mahamevnawa, "Receiving a Blessing Thread."

17. Cavanagh, "Sai Sin and the Sacred White Thread."

18. Bentor, *Consecration of Images and Stupas in Indo-Tibetan Tantric Buddhism*, 102.

pray. Then the hollow is sealed.[19] I obtained the statue from a Seattle Buddhist supply shop where the proprietor told me the white thread wrapped around the wrist of the statue signifies that it has been spiritually activated by Buddhist monks.

If you visit the Shinto temple of the Tsubaki Grand Shrine of North America in Granite Falls in Washington State, you will see a large rope tied around the trunk of a gigantic tree. The rope is called a *shimenawa,* and they are used to mark places where *kami* (gods and spirits of the Shinto religion) are likely to gather or dwell.[20] There are many shimenawa on the grounds, hanging over the path down to the river, suspended above doorways, wrapped around rocks, and hanging over the walkways. They mark where the kami walk from the river to the shrine and back again. Shimenawa can also be used to mark off ritual space, making whatever is enclosed within it sacred ground.[21] This seems to me to be similar to the use of the Witch's cord in casting a circle.

Witches and Pagans use cords too. Part of the Witchcraft initiation ceremony involves taking the initiate's measure.[22] The candidate is laid on the ground and a single thread is measured out from their head to their feet. This measure symbolizes the new Witch's commitment to the vows taken at initiation and serves as a representation of the initiate to which the initiate is magically tied. Some initiators keep the measure and deliver the traditional dire threats about using it in sympathetic magic to dole out punishment if the initiate ever breaks their vows. Other initiators choose to return the

---

19. Bimbaum, "Consecration of Statues and Thangkas."

20. De Garis, *We Japanese,* 197.

21. Yamakage, *The Essence of Shinto,* "Himorogi."

22. Farrar, *The Inner Mysteries.*

measure to the candidate to signal trust and acceptance, returning the responsibility for keeping their commitments to the new Witch.

Some Witches wear braided cords around their waists to signal their lineage and their degree. I am a third-degree Witch in two lines and have two sets of cords, each with three colors; one is white, red, and black, and the second is white, red, and blue. The Witch's cord may be nine feet in length, which makes for a lot of wrapping around the waist. It is this length so it can be used to measure the diameter of a nine-foot circle for the Witch to work in. I held to this practice in my first year as a young Witch and solemnly used my cord to measure a circle. It was hard to find a space that will take a circle that big! I decided that it was more important to me to have a workable space than a by-the-numbers practice, so now I mark a circle in the size I need wherever it will fit.

Pagans also use ropes to tie hands together in a wedding ceremony. The custom of handfasting has moved out from the Pagan community into general use. There are websites that describe how to braid the cord with suggestions on how to decorate it. I've officiated at weddings for Buddhists, magicians, Witches, and non-denominational folk, and every ceremony has included a handfasting cord! It is such a tangible and elegant way to mark the joining of two lives. Just a note to the couple and the officiant: it's a good idea to practice the procedure ahead of time so the process flows smoothly during the wedding itself. It's not difficult but it can be awkward to get the rope around two sets of wrists until you get used to the size of the rope and the size of the hands.

People around the world use threads and ropes to protect newborns, tie newlyweds together, wish the deceased a good next life, deliver a blessing to people in need, remind themselves to pray and connect to their spiritual traditions, carry the power of a deity or temple, and mark places where spirits reside. This is not an exhaustive list—cords have been used for almost any magical purpose imaginable.

Cord Magic is String Plus Magic

String is so useful that it is one of our oldest tools. Even before we made knives to cut things, we were twisting fibers. Before string, we had to carry everything in our hands. Our ancestors used twine to make handles and bags to hold objects. The bags could be tied around the neck and waist and free up hands for gathering plants and carrying babies. Twine could be made into nets to catch small game. Ropes could be used to hang bags and plants and small game from tree limbs and stone outcroppings to form natural hooks.

Today, string is still one of the most useful tools around the house. In the garden, a ball of twine ties up sagging plants, attaches tomato vines to stakes, provides a support for climbing peas, and bundles herbs to hang them to dry. Kitchen twine can truss up chicken and meat roasts, hang onions, or tie a bouquet of herbs in soup.

In the summertime, clotheslines can air out laundry in the fresh breeze. Rope looped into a hole can hang a pot or spoon. Rope wrapped around a dowel can suspend a tapestry from a wall.

Decorative cords have many uses in handcrafts. They can tie up packages, make drawstrings for bags, or hang a pendant. Craft magazines, websites, and videos give instructions on how to make cords in simple and complicated patterns.

String is such a useful device that we naturally reach for it when we have a need for magic too. The basic function of a string is to tie things together and hang things from ourselves. When we add an intention, the cord becomes a way to tie magic onto something or someone. None of the things we use string for in our daily lives is magical in itself. Any can be turned into magical acts by adding a blessing to the string.

Now that we've surveyed some of the ways people have used string to create magic, we can jump in and learn how to make our own cords in just minutes using the natural properties of twisted string.

two
Making a Cord

This chapter covers the how-to part of making cords. We'll talk about measuring threads and how to twist them into cords. You can make short cords or longer ones, and you can do it yourself or bring in friends to help. In making the twist, you will take into consideration whether you want to draw the magical energy toward you or to send it out into the world. In addition to colored thread, you can add metal, wood, and stone to your cord talismans in the form of pendants and beads.

The cords in this book all use the twist method to create the cord. Anyone who is able to hold yarn can make a twisted cord. The technique requires just a tiny bit of skill and learning but is easy to pick up. Kids make twisted cords on the first try. Before we start twisting yarn, it can help to understand a little about how thread is spun and rope is plied.

Spinning Thread

Every piece of thread we use needs to be spun. Lucky for us, the yarn and floss we normally use has already been spun. The process of taking a piece of wool or flax that is short and weak and turning it into a thread that is continuous and strong brings the first energy to the material.

Thread is created by spinning short lengths of plant or animal fiber into a continuous strand. Have you ever seen a person hand spinning? It's mesmerizing. One hand feeds the fibers into the thread while the other keeps the drop spindle turning. The thread lengthens in front of your eyes—it's a magical thing to watch in itself.

There is so much commercial and hand-spun yarn available that we never need to spin our own. If you're interested in making your own thread, it's an accessible craft that is relatively easy to learn and great fun to do with friends. Hand spinning requires a drop spindle, which is fairly inexpensive. Spinning can also be mechanized with a spinning wheel. A wheel is definitely an investment, but make for beautiful pieces that are quite dramatic in appearance. When I walk into a living room and see a spinning wheel in the corner, I know I'm in the presence of a fiber artist. Yarn stores and weaving guilds offer classes in drop spinning and spinning wheels, and there are many books and online videos to show you the basics.

The Shape of the Twist

Here's a bit of technical information about how spinning shapes thread. The yarn you buy actually has a twist already. It turns out that the twist has a direction and a name.

Whether spinning by hand or on a wheel, thread has to turn in a single direction or the fibers won't spin properly. If you're right-handed and spinning by hand, you will automatically turn the spindle clockwise. This creates a twist called the *right twist* or Z *twist*, because when you look closely at it, the fibers seem to lay around the thread core in the shape of the letter z. A counterclockwise twist is called a left twist or S twist because the fibers take the shape of the letter s.[23]

S and Z Twists

While fiber folk love learning about this kind of thing, it's not necessary for you to remember or have a deep understanding about this. What's important to our magic is the idea that spinning is the foundation of cord magic and the very first twist. This material becomes a cord talisman when we work with it and bless it.

Measuring Thread

The first step in working with a cord is to measure the thread. You can of course use a ruler to lay out a length of string, but you can also use your own body to quickly calculate the material you

---

23. Austin, *Hand Spinning*, "S or Z?"

need. Before yardsticks and tape measures, people used body parts to estimate lengths. If you've been around horses, you know their height is measured in hands. Fabric sellers measure cloth by the yard. Sailors check the depth of water in fathoms.

Here's the list of body part measurements.[24]

Quick Reference
MEASUREMENTS

Inch: the width of the thumb.

Hand or palm: the width of the palm.

Span: the length of the hand from the wrist to the end of the middle finger.

Foot: the length of the foot from the heel to end of the big toe.

Cubit: the length of the forearm from the elbow to the end of the middle finger.

Yard: the length measured from the nose to the middle fingertip of the outstretched arm.

Fathom: the length of outstretched arms from one middle fingertip to the other.

This is the origin of the inch, foot, and yard. As these measurements became standardized over time, they became somewhat larger than they started. For example, there aren't many feet that are actually twelve inches! Your measurements are likely to be shorter than the standard measurements listed in the table that follows.

---

24. Klein, *The Science of Measurement*, 54–68.

You may decide to measure out your thread length meticulously using measuring tape or yardsticks. If you know how to use your own measurements, it's much quicker and you always have your measuring tools on hand. It's also helpful to know how your body maps out onto the standard measurements. Then you will know why your cords are always a little bit longer or shorter than expected. For example, the length of my yard is 31 inches, not 36.

Below is the first worksheet. The worksheets throughout this book let you collect your own information to design your cords. For this worksheet, you measure yourself to find your own measurements. You can use a tape measure to measure yourself or ask a friend to take the measurements (the latter is easier and a bit more accurate).

Worksheet
MEASURE YOURSELF

Unit	Inches	My Measurement
Inch	1	
Hand	4	
Span	9	
Foot	12	
Cubit	18	
Yard	36 (three feet)	
Fathom	72 (six feet)	

My cubit is 16 inches, my yard is about 31 inches, and my fathom is about 67 inches. I have short arms! When I measure threads for cord magic, I make the lengths about two inches longer than my cubit to compensate.

Now that you have your measurements, you're ready to make your first cord.

Single-thread Cords

The simplest form of cord magic is a single colored string. With a dyed string, you can make a blessing. For single-thread cord magic, you can use embroidery floss, knitting yarn, or even kitchen or garden twine in a pinch. The important thing is that the material you choose has meaning for you.

You can use any material you already own. Fabric and craft suppliers carry a widely colored variety of yarn and embroidery floss. Many small home craft businesses sell hand-spun and hand-dyed wool and even linen. You might even find a yarn section in your local grocery-and-home-goods store.

The material you use can be any size of thread or yarn. A thinner thread such as embroidery floss is more fragile but easier to conceal. Yarn comes in several sizes from very fine to bulky. A medium weight works best for cord you will wear on your wrist or to hold a pendant.

Charm
RED THREAD PROTECTION

For this spell, use a red string. To create the cord you will measure, cleanse, bless, and tie the string.

Measure: First, measure the length of the string. For this rite use a cubit, which is the length of your forearm from the elbow to the tip of your middle finger, or 18 inches.

Cleanse: Next, sprinkle it with water. Say, "This cord is cleansed by water to be fit for my purpose."

Bless: Hold the string between your hands. Say, "This cord protects me and blesses me." If it is meant to be a gift, substitute the name of the recipient: "This cord protects (name) and blesses (name)."

Tie: The binding is complete when the two ends are knotted together. How to wear it:

- Ask a friend to tie it around your wrist, wrapping it a few times and tying a knot
- Knot it yourself and wear it around your neck
- Place it in a small bag and carry it in your pocket or handbag

To give as a gift: Wrap it in tissue, place it in a small box or bag, and write out a card with your blessing for the receiver.

Using a red cord for protection is nearly universal. Why red? It's the color of blood. The infant in the womb is tied to the mother through a blood cord. Blood makes our skin rosy while we are alive. Wounded soldiers bleed on the battlefield. Red is the color of life. When a red string is closed it makes a circle, a protective device in nearly every human culture.

Charm
DIVINE BLESSING

You can use a single thread to carry the blessings of deities. If you have ever participated in the Hindu ceremony called puja, you may have seen this ritual in practice. During it, the participants sometimes place red and gold threads on the statues of the deities, and then take those threads and wear them when the ritual is complete.

For this rite, you invite the divine presence into a physical space, an altar, which may include a picture or statue of the deity. The rite "charges" or transfers energy from the altar to the cord.

Select the deity: This can be a goddess, god, or other deity you already know. You can also use this as an opportunity to establish a closer relationship with a deity.

Choose the cord: As with the single cord blessing, you can use any yarn or embroidery floss you already own, or you can purchase a new skein. The string can be any size. The color can be any color that you know the deity is associated with. If you're not sure, you can always use red. Measure and cut about 18 inches of the material, or about a forearm's length.

Set up the altar: On a small table or shelf, set up a statue or picture of the deity. Place a small candle in front of the statue and have a lighter nearby. Place the cord you have measured on the altar.

Invoke the deity: Sit yourself in front of the altar. Take three deep breaths. See and feel yourself connected to the earth. Now focus on the statue or picture. Place your hands together at your heart center and bow slightly. Say, "(Name of deity), please be present here with me." See and feel a light settling on the image. The light can be golden or can be the color that you have chosen for the cord.

Commune with the deity: Now you can talk with the deity to ask for a specific wish, such as protection or health, or to ask for general blessings. You can also thank the deity for their presence in your life.

Charge the cord: Place the length of cord on the picture or statue. Say, "(Name of deity), please bless me." See and feel the light on the image soaking into the cord.

Release the deity: Place your hands together at your heart center and bow slightly. Say, "(Name of deity), thank you for your presence."

Carry the thread: Wear the thread around your wrist and knot it, carry it next to your skin, or place it in a pocket or handbag.

In Hindu ritual, the deity is usually presented with an offering. You can optionally make this part of the ritual as well. Offerings include liquids (water and wine), food (small plates of fruit, cheese, and sweets), and incense. If you don't have the space or time to make a physical offering, you can imagine yourself making the offerings. The important thing is to make the offering with a sincere heart.

If you are wearing the string around your wrist, you can wear it until it falls off. In practice, this can take a long time. As an alternative, when you're ready to stop wearing it, you can carefully slip it over your hand. Try to avoid cutting it off if at all possible, as this spills out the energy of the cord. If you have to do it, see and feel the deity in front of you and say, "Thank you for your blessings."

Twisted Cords

We've been talking about single-strand cord magic. When using multiple threads, they must be combined in some way, and the simplest way is to twist them together.

Here's the simple explanation: twist two or more threads together until they start to kink. Then fold the threads in half and let go. The threads will twist around each other. Knot the two loose ends together and you're done!

The Science of Plying Yarn

Here's some more detail for craftspeople and magical technicians. You can skip down to the next section if you want to move straight to making a cord.

The yarn we buy in a yarn shop is very rarely composed of just one thread; it is almost always at least two-ply. A single thread tends to be fragile, while plying results in a stronger yarn. To ply a yarn, you twist two or more threads together. Here's the neat part: you ply them in the opposite direction from the one in which they were originally spun.

You may remember from the section on spinning thread that each thread has either a Z twist or an S twist. If the thread is a right or Z-twist thread, you ply it counter-clockwise; if the thread is a left or S-twist thread, you ply it clockwise. Because most of us are right-handed, thread is usually spun right and plied left.

Rope making works on the same principle as plying. The rope material, usually hemp or nylon, is twisted then folded back on itself in a spiral helix. The helix rotates in the opposite direction from the original twist.[25]

Ply Creates the Twist

We leverage the physical properties of plying in cord magic. After two or more threads are twisted together, they'll unspin themselves if we let go, even if we knot them at both ends. The trick is folding the twisted cord in half. Now the halves mirror each other—the spin on one half is going in the opposite direction from the second half. When you let go, they automatically twine around each other.

---

25. Bohr, "The Ancient Art of Laying Rope."

Rope made from hemp will hold its shape when it is folded against itself, but a small length of twisted yarn will tend to unravel. To prevent this we knot the two ends.

When you fold a twisted cord in half, you've lost half of the length. So you might think that you need to measure twice as much yarn as you need for the final cord length. In practice, however, we measure out *three* times as much yarn as the final cord length. Why?

There is a physical limit to how much thread can be twisted. Technically, this is called the zero-twist configuration. You can tell that you've reached this limit when the cord starts to kink back on itself. When a length of thread has reached the zero-twist configuration, it is exactly 68 percent shorter than it started out. You don't need to remember that; all you need to know is that the twist will reduce the length of the thread by about one-third.

To recap: you lose half the length of the thread in folding and another third in twisting. You'll need space for the knot, and if you decide to knot the bent end, you'll lose some length there as well.

> **Tip:** Measure out lengths of yarn that are three times as long as the finished cord. You'll end up with a little bit more than you need, which is easy to cut off—just make a knot where you want the final length and cut off the excess.

Exercise

TWIST A CORD

This technique creates a cord in minutes.

Measure: First, measure the threads. As mentioned in the previous section, each thread should be about three times the desired end length of the cord. So if you are making a one-foot cord, the individual threads need to be three feet long. Unless otherwise noted, the cords in this book call for threads that are a yard (36 inches), or about the length from your outstretched fingertip to your nose.

Lay out the threads, from two to as many as you like. Using more threads makes a thicker cord. Tie the threads together at each end in a knot. When you lay it out, you will have a length of cords bound together with a knot at both ends.

Tie: Tie one end to a sturdy object like a table leg or drawer handle with a loose overhand knot you'll be able to untie later. Another option is to tie a tight knot on the drawer handle, then tie another knot fairly close to it. To release the completed cord, cut between the two knots, then clean up the knot on the drawer handle by working it loose or cutting through it. You can also tie the threads onto one end of an S-hook and use the other end to hook onto a drawer handle.

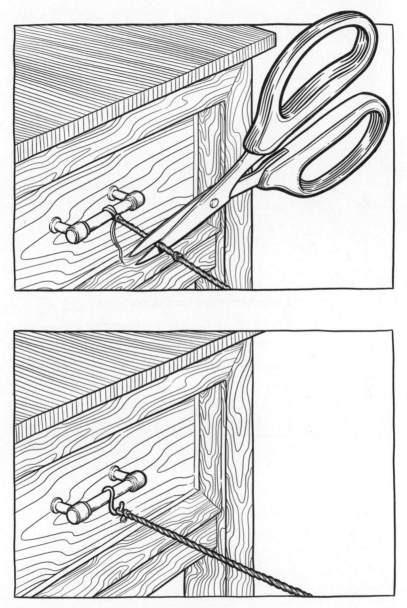

Tie

Twist: Step back until the threads are stretched out to their full length. Taking the farthest knot into your hands and keeping the threads tight, turn the cord in your hands. The threads will begin to wind together. As they wind, you will notice increasing tension in the wound threads. Eventually, it will begin to kink on itself. That's the signal that it's been twisted enough.

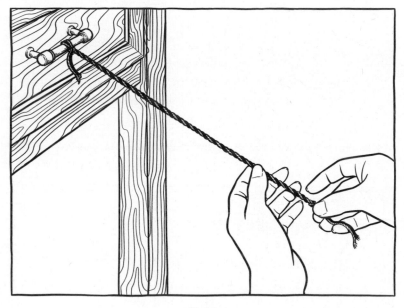

Twist

Fold: Grasp the cord halfway up its length in one hand. Maintaining the tension on the cord, bring the second knot back to the knot tied to the table leg or drawer handle. Hold the two knotted ends together in one hand. Now you've halved the cord. In one hand, you hold the two knotted ends; in the other, you hold an unknotted end (a loop). Don't drop it yet! It might take a practice session or two to learn how to bring the two knotted ends together and keep them from twisting before you're ready.

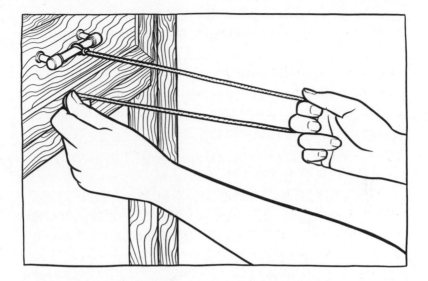

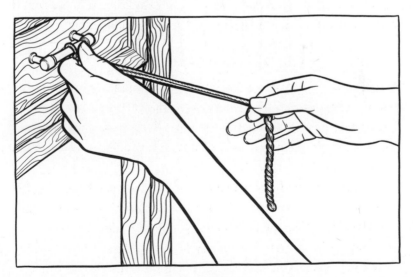

Fold

Still holding the two knotted ends together, let go of the unknotted end. The cord will twist itself together. If you've twisted the thread until it kinked, this can happen in the blink of an eye!

Untie and knot end: Smooth the cord out so the tension is even along its length. Untie the knotted end from the object that was holding it. Tie a new knot on that end around the original knots to keep the twist together.

That's it—you've made your cord!

If you've never done this before, you can use inexpensive or scrap yarn to practice. Doing it just a few times will teach you how to manage the tension to make a tighter or looser cord. In general, you will want to keep the cord tight enough by keeping a firm grip on the cord and pulling it firmly away from the anchor point. You can distribute the tension along the cord by holding it in one hand and stroking back toward the anchor point with the other.

The Direction of the Energy

Spinning fiber imparts energy into the thread. Plying imparts energy into it as well. That energy has physical properties that can be measured, such as tenacity (how much force it takes to break the thread), ply security (how well does it stay plied), and elasticity (how stretchy is the thread).

When we twist threads together, we add energy which results in a cord that is physically stronger but less elastic than the original thread. It is also the first chance you have to direct that energy magically. You can send the energy of the cord out from yourself or inward toward yourself. For the purposes of this book, you will send energy out when you are working to manifest something or bring it to yourself, as in prosperity work. You will keep energy in when you are working to hold energy close, as in protection magic.

Exercise

SENDING ENERGY OUT AND KEEPING ENERGY IN

Measure three threads. Tie one end to a drawer handle using a slip-knot or S-hook. You can twist the thread in this position, turning either to the right or to the left—right sends the energy out, left keeps the energy in. You can also turn your body so that you are holding the thread perpendicular to your body. Now you can twist the thread toward you or away from you.

Sending energy out: Twist the thread right or away from you. Say, "I send this energy out into the world." You can say this once as you start the twist, or repeat it until the twist is complete.

Keeping energy in: Twist the thread left or toward you. Say, "This energy circles me and protects me." You can say this once as you start the twist, or repeat it until the twist is complete.

When the twist is complete, fold the cord and knot the ends. As you make the knot, say, "This cord is sealed."

Twisting with Two People

Twisting a cord with another person was the first way I learned to make a cord. It's the quickest and easiest method because you don't have to find a stable object to hold one end of the cord, and you don't have to make a slip knot or find an S-hook. This method also lets you make a longer cord than you can make on your own.

Exercise
TWO-PERSON TWIST

You can ask a friend to help you make a cord for yourself, or you and your cord-making partner may decide to make a cord that you will divide, so each of you can have the magic.

Measure: Measure the threads and knot them on each end. Hold one knotted end and have your partner hold the other. Step away from each other until the threads are fairly taut.

Twist: Are you sending the energy out or keeping it in? Once you have decided, turn your body sideways to your partner. Each of you faces in the opposite direction. Both of you begin to twist the thread either toward yourself or away from yourself. Both of you must twist in the same direction—if one of you turns toward yourself and the other person turns away, the cord won't wind.

Fold: When the cord begins to kink, have your partner stand still. Grasp the middle of the cord and walk your knotted end over to theirs, and put the two knotted ends together, being careful to keep the threads tight. Have your partner hold the knotted ends together. Walk your end of the cord out to stretch it to its full length. Now let go of your end, and warn your partner to keep holding onto the knotted ends. The cord will wind itself up automatically.

Knot: Tie the two knotted ends together to secure the cord.

Making Longer Cords

You might want to make a really long cord to use as a belt or trim on clothing, or to make a circle around an object or a room. When making a cord by yourself, you are more or less limited to using threads that measure a fathom (the length of your outstretched arms, about six feet). The end result will be a cord a little longer than two feet. Working with a partner will allow you to make longer cords.

Folding a long thread is a little trickier than folding a shorter one. If a cord touches the ground, it no longer twists properly. So if your cord length exceeds the height at which you can hold your hands above your head, you will need to find a place such as a staircase or step-stool to give you the height to hang the cord at its full length.

With a long cord, don't let go of the thread all at once; it may not twist properly. To make sure the cord winds smoothly, you can twist it in stages. Hold a length of the cord in both hands, then let go of the hand closest to the knot end while hanging on with the hand closer to the folded end. Keep "walking" up the cord until you've twisted the entire length. With a longer cord, you may want to smooth the length of the cord to ensure the twist is evenly distributed.

If you want to make a really long cord, you'll need to add one more person. Here's how to add the extra person to the process.

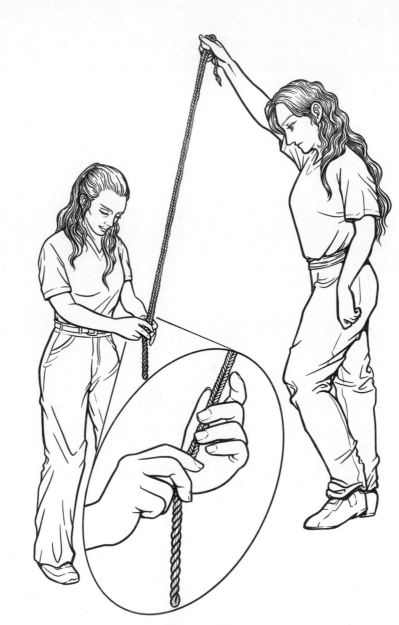

Long Cord Twist

Exercise
THREE-PERSON TWIST

Measure: Measure the threads and knot them on each end. You hold one knotted end and your partner holds the other end. Step away from each other until the threads are fairly taut.

Twist: Are you sending the energy out or keeping it in? Once you have decided, turn your body sideways to your partner. Each of you faces in the opposite direction. Both of you begin to twist the thread either toward yourself or away from yourself. Both of you must twist in the same direction—if one of you turns toward yourself and the other person turns away, the cord won't wind.

Fold: When the cord begins to kink, the third person steps in. Give the end you are holding to the third person. Now position yourself in the middle of the cord and hold on to the cord. Have your two partners walk toward each other until the two knotted ends meet.

Knot: Tie the two knotted ends together to secure the cord.

Exercise
SHARING A CORD BY DIVIDING IT

If you have decided to share the magic, here's how to divide it. Find the middle of the cord, then make two secure knots close to each other. Now cut in between the knots.

Can more people create a cord together? Sure, you can add as many people as you like. I've made a cord with five people; we used the length of the house to stretch out the cord. A group of people might decide to make a cord for a friend as a gift for protection or healing.

Adding Pendants and Beads to a Cord

Have you ever bought a pendant from a crafter at a fair? The jeweler might provide a length of black satin to hang the pendant. Instead of plain cord, some jewelers make twisted cords to add a colorful and personalized touch. You can add a pendant to a cord too.

Make sure the pendant has a jump ring, the small metal loop that attaches to the hole in the pendant. Simply pass the cord through the jump ring. If the jump ring is too small, you can buy a larger one at a craft store or online and replace it. Tie the cord, slip it over your neck, and you're done!

If you want to get extra fancy, you can buy crimp clasps from a craft supply source. Using these clasps allows you to pick your favorite type of clasp—hook and eye, lobster, barrel, or magnetic. Pull the knots at each end of the cord as tight as you can, then cut the threads as short as you can without releasing the knot. Insert the knot into the clasp and use pliers to crimp around the knot. This turns your cord talisman into a piece of art.

You can also add beads to a cord before *or* after you twist the cord. Beads that have larger holes can be slid onto the cord after the cord has been twisted. For beads with smaller holes that won't fit over a finished cord, you can slide them onto one of the threads you have measured to create the cord; it will get twisted into the cord. To get the bead onto the thread, use a beading needle or *carefully* dip the end of the thread in the melted top of a wax candle to make a stiff end.

Adding a Crimp Clasp

Adding a bead

Tip: Keep the beads close together on the first third of the strand's length. When the cord is twisted and folded in half, they'll end up in the right place.

Adding beads to a cord brings in the elements of stone, metal, wood, and color to the talisman, all of which can augment the power of the cord. For example, if you're making a birthday gift for a friend, you could add beads of their birthstone. You can add colored beads for the elements and planets. You can also add metal beads, such as silver for the moon and gold for the sun.

It takes much longer to describe how to twist a cord than to actually do it. This is one of the easiest talismans to create; it literally takes only a few minutes to measure and twist the cord. It's so much fun to watch the yarn spin up—it is addicting! Add in experimenting with color and beads and you may find yourself making cords for every magical purpose.

three
Unmaking a Cord

What happens when you no longer need a cord? Perhaps it has served its purpose or has become so worn that you'd like to replace it. The responsible practitioner knows that any magic created must be properly undone. Fortunately, it's even easier to unmake a cord than it is to make one—release the energy and then recycle the cord.

One option is to recycle a cord in your magic. For example, you might add a protection cord to a Witch's bottle or another protective charm. You can braid your old cords together and hang them to remind yourself of the magics you have accomplished. You could also give them to someone who will find them useful.

You may decide that you are completely done with the cord and would prefer to ground the magic. First, you will need to clean off the energy the cord has attracted in its useful life. A protection cord may have picked up negative energy, a healing cord may hold traces of the illness, a cord that has been carried in public may have picked up energy from people who have handled it.

Once the cord is cleaned, you will need to release the magical energy you have twisted into the cord itself. After that point, the materials once again become fiber. If the thread itself is valuable (e.g., thread made of gold), you might want to keep it for reuse. You may also choose to reuse the cord material in a commitment to recycling or to save money buying new yarn. If the material is worn or if you prefer to move it out of your life altogether, you can dispose of it the same way you handle any worn fabric. You can collect bits of fabric to stuff pillows and toys. One option is to donate old fabric to used clothing stores that will recycle them into rags. Throwing fiber materials in the garbage is a last resort, as they will end up in a landfill where they will take a long time to decompose.

Exercise
RELEASE A CORD

Clean:

1. Set out a container of water. If you can, use a container with a lid so you can carry the water later.

2. Sprinkle salt in the water. Stir the salt into the water with your hands three times, saying, "Water and salt cleanses and grounds."

3. Now lay the cord in the water and say, "May you be cleaned of all energy which you have gathered."

4. Set the bowl aside for a day.

5. To avoid contacting the energy that is now in the water, fish out the cord with a tool, a pair of tongs, or even a pencil. Lay the cord on a paper towel.

6. Carry the water outside and pour it into the ground.

Untwist: Cut off the knotted ends of the cord, saying, "You have served your purpose, be released into the world." Smooth out the threads and untangle them until they are once again separate.

Recycle the threads: If you'd like to recycle the threads, here are some options.

1. Keep them to use in other magical projects.

2. Collect them to stuff small plush toys and craft projects.

3. Add them to a thrift store donation bag with clothes you are donating.

We've looked at some of the history of cord talismans, ways to create cords, and how to unmake them when their work is done. Now it's time to dive into the exciting world of designing cords to meet specific magical needs, using color, number, fiber, and most importantly of all, intention.

Part 2
Cord Magic Design

Magic workers are not the only people who make cords. Craftspeople twist cords to hang pendants or ornaments, and fabric workers use them to make edging on knitted or woven fabrics. So what's the difference between a crafted cord and a magical cord? What sets the magical cord apart?

The difference is in how the cord is made. After all, you're doing more than creating something pretty as a decoration. Using your knowledge of magic to make thoughtful choices in every step of the process, you will build your purpose into the cord as you go. You cut yarn of one or more colors into a given number of lengths. The color, number of strands, and fabric are all choices you make that have magical significance. Each choice can harmonize with the cord's overall purpose.

In the next four chapters, we will explore each design choice in depth. Many cultures and magical systems assign meaning to color and numbe; we will review a few of these as examples. At each step you will fill out a worksheet that captures your own associations. Use these to fill in the design template. Once it is complete, you can use the template in a project to create and magically charge a cord.

Here are the steps in designing a cord.

1. Define the purpose.

2. Choose a number or combination of numbers.

3. Choose a color or combination of colors.

4. Choose the material.

5. Decide how the cord will be worn or tied.

Once the cord is designed, making it takes just a few minutes, and your cord is done.

four
Number

To design a cord, we must first decide how many strands to use. If you just want a quick number for your cord design, use three strands. However, the number of strands in the cord can add another layer of meaning to the design. We can use numerology to align the intention of the cord with the number of the person who will use it. We can also tap into common magical associations.

There is no universal meaning for magical symbols. Meanings vary culturally and change over time. Where we find similarities between cultures, we often find that those cultures were connected through trade and travel, even in very ancient times over long distances. That said, there is one thing that almost all humans have in common: we have ten fingers and ten toes. For that reason, most numbering systems count up to ten. If you're one of the rare humans who has more or less fingers or toes, that's also part of the human experience, and you can use that number to truly personalize your cord.

For practical purposes, we will use between one and nine strands. Thinner threads require more strands to make good-sized cords; thicker threads get bulky fairly quickly. Three strands give enough bulk to be noticeable and also offer an opportunity to work with three colors, making it a good number to use if you just want to make a quick cord.

Your feelings about numbers can be colored by your feelings about mathematics. Some people love the predictable patterns that mathematics show us, while others were taught to count by rote and resent the rigidity. But numbers are more than ways to make calculations—they also have emotional and psychological effects. When you think about it, you may find that numbers do have meaning for you. For example, one means independence, two means relationship, four means stability. Before we look at the meanings of numbers in magical systems, take a moment to jot down your personal thoughts.

Worksheet
MY NUMBER MEANINGS

Number	Meaning
1	
2	
3	
4	
5	
6	

Number	Meaning
7	
8	
9	

For example, here are my personal values. One is unity, two is partnership, three is movement, four is stability, and five is dynamic energy. Then I begin to think of numbers as multiples. Six is 2 x 3, which is partnership plus movement. One way I understand that is through the hermetic idea "as above, so below." Seven is the number of the planets known to the ancients. Eight is 2 x 4, stability plus partnership. Finally, nine is 3 x 3, the perfect expression of the unfolding of movement.

There are no wrong or right answers—whatever the numbers mean is totally up to you. You can use the meaning of the number to strengthen the intention of the cord. If I am making a cord for a new place to live, I can use my meaning of four for stability and use four strands and four colors in the cord. If I am looking for a place to live with a partner, I can use eight strands, stability plus partnership. Or I can make a four-strand cord and attach two beads for the two people who will live there.

For quick reference, here is summary of some general number meanings.

Quick Reference
NUMBER MEANINGS

Number	Meaning	Shape
1	Unity	Point
2	Partnership	Line
3	Creation	Triangle
4	Completion	Square
5	Spirit	Pentacle
6	Spirit in matter	Hexagram, two triangles
7	Planets	Heptagram, seven-pointed star
8	Wheel	Ogdoad, compass wheel
9	Magic	Ennead, three by three

Our Relationship to Number

Do you know your number? Numerology is one of the oldest magical arts. The Chaldean mathematicians of Babylonian mapped numbers to spiritual energies.[26] The Greek philosopher Pythagoras saw the order of the cosmos in geometrical shapes. Magic workers still use the Chaldean and Pythagorean numerology systems.

The art of numerology reveals insights into your personality, work choices, and relationships with lovers, family, and friends. Diving into the system yields fascinating insights. It's beyond the scope of this book to explore them here, but if you are interested in learning more, the bibliography lists several great introductions,

---

26. Lagan, *Chaldean Numerology for Beginners*, "Introduction."

including Gerie Bauer's *Numerology for Beginners* and Heather Alicia Lagan's *Chaldean Numerology for Beginners*.

You may have had your natal chart drawn up by an astrologer, which shows the planets in the sky at the time you were born. This chart indicates the circumstances that will shape your path in life. It is up to you to discover how your own personal life journey will unfold and what you will make of the influences surrounding you at your birth. The "Cord Magic Projects" section includes some ideas about using astrological associations in cords.

You can also explore your birth influences through numerology. You can find your personal number using your birth date and your given name at birth. Both of these will show you aspects of your personality in the context of your birth circumstances. If you have changed your name, you can use your new name to trace how your personality has developed over the course of your life.

Exercise
FIND YOUR BIRTH DATE NUMBER

If you already know your birth date number, you can skip to the next section. If you don't, it's easy to find. Add the numbers of the year, month, and day of your birth. Keep adding them together until you arrive at a single digit.

First, add the numbers in your year of birth together. If you were born in 2001, add 2+0+0+1 to get 3. Next add the numbers of your birth month together. January through September give the numbers 1–9, October is 1+0 which is 1, November is 1+1 which is 2, and December is 1+2 which is 3. Finally, add the numbers of your birth day together. For example, if you were born on the 22nd you would add 2+2 to get 4.

A person born on December 22, 2001, would have a year number of 3, a month number of 3, and a day number of 6. Adding these together, 3+3+6=12. Taken down to a single digit, we add 1+2 to get 3.

Exercise

FIND YOUR BIRTH NAME NUMBER

If you already know your birth name number, you can skip to the next section. If not, here's how to find the number of your name. Use the Pythagorean number chart to add up the letters of your first and last name. Here is how to calculate "Jane Smith." For "Jane" you add 1+1+5+5 to get 12, and 1+2 to get 3. "Smith" is 1+4+9+2+8 which totals 24, and 2+4 is 6. Now add 3+6 to get 9. You may choose to add your middle name if you use it in daily life, e.g., "Mary Jane."

Pythagorean Number Chart

1	2	3	4	5	6	7	8	9
A	B	C	D	E	F	G	H	I
J	K	L	M	N	O	P	Q	R
S	T	U	V	W	X	Y	Z	

If Jane Smith was born on December 22, 2001, her birth date number is 3 and her birth name number is 9. One way to think about it is that the birth date number shows us the original personality framework, and the birth name number shows us the personal development goal we have in our lifetime. Our birth date shows us who we were starting out, and our birth name number shows us who we are becoming. Studying your personal numbers can show your strengths and flaws.

What follows is a very simple chart providing the traits of each number.

Quick Reference
PERSONAL NUMBER TRAITS[27]

Number	Character	Strength	Flaw
1	Leader	Gets things done	Arrogant
2	Helpmate	Gets along with everyone	Lets others dominate them
3	Creative	Artistic and entertaining	Scattered
4	Builder	Solidly responsible	Rigid
5	Adventurer	Open to new experiences	Addiction
6	Peace-maker	Nurturing and kind	Overcommits
7	Thinker	Seeker after truth	Critical
8	Visionary	Generous and ambitious	Shuts others out
9	Sensitive	Cares about the world	Unforgiving

---

27. These quick associations are the result of my experience and studies. The sources I rely on are Bauer, Larock, and Maanasvi—my personal favorite. I strongly recommend exploring one of those references in more depth.

Since we know Jane Smith was born on 12/22/2001, making her a 3, we can expect that she is a creative person. She likes to make things and loves being with her friends. She does have a tendency to be scattered, which leads her to be late to her dates. We also know that her name makes her a 9, so her creative nature is making her more sensitive over time. She might use her art to draw attention to causes she cares about. Because she is so passionate, she tends to be judgmental about other people's choices.

If Jane decided to make a cord to attract new friends, she might choose three strands to leverage her natural friendliness. Her intention could include an affirmation that she will stay grounded and make her appointments. Or she could send out a call for friends who are flexible about time! If Jane's friend Jamar makes a cord as a gift for her, he might choose nine threads to strengthen her developing sensitivity and her commitment to improving the world.

Magical Number Associations

If you are a magic user, you are probably already familiar with the magical use of numbers. Witches honor a triple goddess. Celtic magic works with three elements—sea, sky, and land. Classical Hellenistic magic counts four or five elements: earth, air, fire, and water, forming a square in four directions, along with the fifth element, aether or spirit.

Some of the deities and associations in this section may be new to you. You can skip the ones you don't find meaningful. You may find that some of these names and ideas intrigue you and send you down a whole new path of magical discovery. One of the best things about magic is that you can always learn something new, no matter how long you've been practicing.

Here are some number meanings used by practitioners in various magical communities along with ideas about how to use them in designing a cord.

One: Unity

A single thread is the simplest cord magic. The number one lends itself to meditations on unity, the source of creation, independence, and self-reliance. With a single thread, we can pick a color and speak an intention.

Two: Partnership

This is the first combination. In a practical sense, two lets us bring in different colors and textures to the thread. Two different things forming a unity reminds us of the power of human generation, two people combining egg and sperm to reproduce. It is the number of polarity, opposites that anchor a space or time.

Day	Night
Sky	Earth
Up	Down
Spirit	Matter
Lover	Beloved

We can use two strands in a cord to bring two things together: two people, a person and a place, an individual and a group of people, e.g., a family or club.

Three: Creation

The trinity is the first true multiple. Three includes combination, two things combining to create a third. Here are some examples of threes.

- **Primary colors:** red, blue, yellow
- **Human being:** body, mind, spirit
- **Celtic world:** land, sea, sky
- **Alchemical elements:** salt, sulphur, mercury
- **Egyptian deity families:** Isis, Osiris, Horus (mother, father, son); Khnum, Satis, Anuket (father, mother, daughter)
- **Graces:** Aglaia (Radiance), Euphrosyne (Joy), Thalia (Flowering)
- **Muses:** Melete (practice), Mneme (memory), Aoede (song)
- **Hindu gods:** Brahman, Vishnu, Shiva
- **Hindu goddesses:** Saraswati, Lakshmi and Kali

We can use three strands in a cord to invoke any of these principles. Three is especially effective in handfasting cords where two people join to create a marriage.

Four: Completion

Multiply two by two and you get four, the first square. The square describes the world. The sense of completion lends itself to ideas that describe a complete place or time. Here are some examples:

- **Quadrants of the compass:** east, south, west, north
- **Elements:** air, fire, water, earth
- **Colors:** yellow, red, blue, green

- **Times of day:** dawn, noon, sunset, midnight
- **Seasons:** spring, summer, fall, winter
- **Ages of humans:** childhood, adolescence, adulthood, old age
- **Archangels:** Raphael, Michael, Gabriel, Auriel (or Uriel)
- **Temperaments or Humors:** sanguine, choleric, melancholic, phlegmatic
- **Greek winds:** Eurus, Notus, Zephyrus, Boreas

Nearly all these fours have been placed at one time or another on the quartered compass to form a symbolic description of the universe. For example, east can be air, yellow, and spring all at once.

East: air, yellow, spring

South: fire, red, summer

West: water, blue, fall

North: earth, green, winter

Four strands in a cord can evoke all the associations of quarters, with red calling in the powers of the south, fire, summer, and so on for all the colors.

Five: Spirit

Five is a prime number, which means it is not the result of multiplying any other numbers together. Like the trinity, five can represent unity, i.e., four things combining to create a fifth. Four elements plus spirit make up the pentacle.

- **Compass:** east, south, west, north, center
- **Elements:** air, fire, water, earth, spirit
- **Human senses:** sight, hearing, smell, taste, touch

Each of these can be placed on the points of the pentacle. The shape of the pentacle can also be seen as a human body, as in Leonardo Da Vinci's drawing of the Vitruvian Man.

We can add another color to a four-strand cord to represent the fifth element, for example adding purple to represent spirit.

Six: Spirit in Matter

A hexagram is a six-sided figure. Sometimes this is represented as two interlocking triangles, one pointing upward and the other pointing downward. Together, they form a symbol of spirit. The downward triangle manifests in matter, and the upward triangle reaches to spirit.

Six can be any two iterations of three, or the result of adding two to four. Six is also the number of the sides of a cube.

- **Directions:** north, east, south, west, up, down
- **Elements:** air, fire, water, earth, spirit, matter
- **Surfaces:** front, back, right, left, above, below
- **Primary and secondary colors:** red, yellow, and blue; orange, green, and purple
- **Rainbow colors:** red, orange, yellow, green, blue, violet

We can add a sixth strand to a five-strand cord to bring in the additional element. For example, in a cord with yellow, red, blue, green, and purple for air, fire, water, earth, and spirit, we could add a black yarn to represent matter.

The rainbow has many associations. The LGBTQIA community flies a rainbow flag and rainbow cords can express solidarity and pride.

Seven: Planets

The Pythagorean number system calls seven the perfect number. It is certainly a magic number! There are many sets of seven. The one most commonly used is the set of seven planets known to the ancients.

- **Places:** seven seas, seven heavens, seven hells, seven wonders of the world
- **Planets:** the sun, Mercury, Venus, the moon, Mars, Jupiter, Saturn

  Egyptian and Babylonian astronomers detected seven planets, stars that did not stay fixed in place but instead wandered across the sky. The planets are associated with the points of the star with seven rays.
- **Days of the week:** Monday/moon, Tuesday/Mars, Wednesday/Mercury, Thursday/Jupiter, Friday/Venus, Saturday/Saturn

  Each planet rules a day, thus giving seven days of the week
- **Directions:** north, south, east, west, center, and up and down

  Some magical traditions invoke seven elements, creating a three-dimensional box or sphere of energy.
- **Musical scale:** c, d, e, f, g, a, b

  The musical scale demonstrates the mathematical ratios that govern the cosmos and create the music of the spheres.
- **Spectrum colors:** red, orange, yellow, green, blue, indigo, violet

Isaac Newton used a prism to split sunlight into the primary and secondary colors. He added indigo to the rainbow to bring the number of colors to the magic seven.

We could use seven different shades of blue to create a seven seas cord, blue and yellow to create a seven heavens cord, or add in green to create a seven wonders cord. Instead of a cord representing seven "hells," we could create a cord representing the seven gates to the underworld in shades of red and orange.

For a cord representing seven directions, we could use one color of choice or assign seven different colors. That cord would be a good basis for a safety rite, creating a sphere of protection around the person or place.

Eight: Wheel

Eight is two sets of four. When the directions and the seasons double, they create the wheel. The cardinal directions blossom into the compass rose. The four seasons expand into the wheel of the year.

Another name for a set of eight is the ogdoad. Eight is the number of the places where the lines of the cube meet (vertices).

- **Directions:** east, southeast, south, southwest, west, northwest, north, northeast
- **Greek winds:** Eurus, Apeliotes, Notus, Livos, Zephyrus, Skiron, Boreas, Kaikias
- **Sabbats:** Imbolc, Beltane, Ostara, Lammas, Mabon, Samhain, Yule
- **Egyptian Hermopolitan Ogdoad:** Nu and Naunet (water), Kuk and Kauket (darkness), Hu and Hauhet (space), Amun and Amaunet (creation)

- **Eight colors:** red, orange, yellow, green, blue, purple, white, black
- **New rainbow flag:** red, orange, yellow, green, blue, violet, brown, black
  The new LGBTQIA rainbow flag adds the colors brown and black to include people of color.

Just as two creates polarity and four creates a square, eight creates a compass. We can divide a square or circle into eight sections to describe the eight directions. The sabbats laid out on the compass create the wheel of the year.

Creating cords with eight strands, we can use one color to represent the set or eight colors to represent each of the specific energies in the set. We can also build on the idea of sets of twos and fours. For the directions, we might use yellow for east, red for south, blue for west, and green for north, and then a color in between for the other directions: orange for southeast, reddish-blue for southwest, blue-green for northwest, and yellowish-green for northeast.

Nine: Magic

Nine is the number of magic. It contains the power of all the numbers before the new set begins with ten. It is three times three, multiplying the power of each number three times. A shape with nine sides or a set of nine items is an ennead.

- **Greek Muses:** Calliope (epic poetry), Clio (history), Euterpe (lyric poetry), Thalia (comedy), Melpomene (tragedy), Terpsichore (dance), Erato (love poetry), Polyhymnia (sacred poetry), Urania (astronomy)

- **Egyptian Heliopolitan Ennead:** Atum, Shu, Tefnut, Geb, Nut, Osiris, Set, Isis, Nepthys

- **Norse (worlds):** Asgard, Alfheimr, Niovellir, Midgard, Jotunheimr, Vanaheimr, Niflheim, Muspelheim, Hel

- **Nine colors:** red, orange, yellow, green, blue, indigo, violet, white, black

To create cords with nine strands, we can use one color, three strands each of three colors, or nine different colors. Nine is at the practical limit for the size of a cord and for managing the associations.

Now that we've looked at numerology and magical number associations, this is a good time to revisit the worksheet "My Number Associations." Do you have new thoughts about some of the numbers?

As you can see, one of the most important ways we express numbers in designing a cord is by choosing colors to represent them. Color is the next design element we will explore.

five
Color

olor is one of the most fascinating tools in the magical tool-kit. For cord magic specifically, color is one of the most important design decisions we can make.

The meanings of colors vary culturally and change over time. Which colors are the right ones to use? The most important answer is: any colors you choose will be the right ones. That said, color has developed cultural meaning from the shades found in nature, the frequencies of light, the history of dyes, and the colors of the plan-ets. We will look at these meanings for each of the colors in the magical spectrum.

While numbers can seem abstract and cerebral, color is vis-ceral. Just looking at a blue wall or wearing a red jacket instantly evokes emotion. We know what colors we like to surround our-selves with and what colors we like to wear. We also know what colors and combinations we hate! Before we examine some of the cultural associations with color, take a moment to record your per-sonal associations.

Worksheet
MY COLOR MEANINGS

Color	My Meaning
Red	
Orange	
Yellow	
Green	
Blue	
Lavender	
Purple	
White	
Black	

Your color meanings will be unique to you. Cultures also assign meaning to color, and the language we speak reflects some of these associations. A loyal friend is true blue, an angry person is "seeing red," a flowery novel is written in purple prose. Magic also assigns meaning to colors through their associations with the elements and the planets.

Entire books have been written about each color of the rainbow; we will briefly explore some of the physical effects of color, including the history of dyes, the physical body of color.

The rainbow provides us with a baseline color palette to create cords. Expanding that palette gives us additional range. Every cord project in this book can be created with the expanded color palette.

For quick reference, here is summary of the color meanings we will explore.

Quick Reference
RAINBOW COLOR PALETTE MEANINGS

Color	Meaning	Element	Planet
Red	Life, sex, love	Fire	Mars
Orange	Excitement	Fire	Mercury
Yellow	Light, happiness	Air	Sun
Green	Earth, healing	Earth	Venus
Blue	Peace, work	Water	Jupiter
Purple	Power, success	Spirit	Moon
White	Neutral	Spirit	Moon
Black	Neutral	Spirit	Saturn

Quick Reference
EXPANDED COLOR PALETTE MEANINGS

Color	Meaning
Light red	Love
Red	Passion
Dark red	Life blood
Light orange	Communication
Orange	Excitement
Dark orange	Protection
Light yellow	Optimism
Yellow	Happiness
Dark yellow	Inspiration

Color	Meaning
Light green	New growth
Green	Health
Dark green	Prosperity
Light blue	Relief
Blue	Peace
Dark blue	Dependability
Light purple	Aspiration
Purple	Power
Dark purple	Success
Red-orange (coral)	Hope
Yellow-orange (amber)	Confidence
Yellow-green (chartreuse)	Imagination
Red-purple (magenta)	Compassion
Blue-green (turquoise)	Wisdom
Blue-purple (periwinkle)	Serenity
Beige	Natural world
Pink	Romantic love
Brown	Support
White	Neutral
Gray	Neutral
Black	Neutral

Our Relationship to Color

What is color?[28] It is:

- a wavelength of light
- a physical property
- a human perception

Sunlight is a wavelength of light. We react to light, and we also react to specific colors. These reactions are physical responses that we can measure. First, the human body needs sunlight.[29] When we stand in sunlight, our skin synthesizes vitamin D, which we need to form strong bones. Exposure to sunlight helps prevent tuberculosis, diabetes, hypertension, and some forms of cancer. Sunlight also regulates our body's production of melatonin, which affects our ability to sleep.

Sunlight contains all the colors of the spectrum. It turns out that our bodies have a physiological reaction to specific colors.[30] Light stimulates the human nervous system, which controls body temperature and blood pressure. Light also affects the glands that regulate hormone production. The manner in which light affects us depends on the light's color. Red light increases blood pressure and stimulates hormone production. Blue light decreases blood pressure and depresses hormone production. That's why we describe red, orange, and yellow as warm and stimulating; and green, blue, and violet as cool and calming.

28. Linda Holtzschue, *Understanding Color*, in "Color as Language, from Name to Meaning."

29. Mead, "Benefits of Sunlight."

30. Linda Holtzschue, *Understanding Color*, in "Physiology, Responding to Light."

Color is a wavelength of light and is also a physical property. It's hard for us today to think of color as a physical property because we make almost any object almost any color. Personally, my wardrobe is a rainbow! I can buy the same pair of pants in rust and brown, navy and gray. My shirts range from bright yellow to somber black. I have sundresses printed with flowers that swirl around the skirt in all the colors of summer.

Before the mid-1880s, the colors of everyday clothing were limited to drab or dull colors. So when a Swedish chemist named Carl Scheele stumbled on a dye that created brilliant green fabric, the Victorian world went mad for it. Throughout the 1800s, Scheele's green showed up in wallpaper, women's dresses and gloves, and even children's clothing. Unfortunately, the dye that created the color contained arsenic—which is poisonous! Putting your hands in that pair of gloves could give you blisters, and brushing up against the wallpaper could make you sick. Scheele himself died of arsenic poisoning at age 43.[31] As popular as it became, Scheele's green dye was banned in the late 1800s.

The story of Scheele's green shows the lengths people have been willing to go to for color. Before the invention of synthetic dyes, bright clothing was hard to come by—our palette was limited to the dyes made from plants, animals, minerals and metals. For example, people commonly extracted blue from woad, yellow from chamomile or onions, purple from snails, red or purple from beets or ground up insects.

When it comes to fabric, color is a physical substance. Dye is the body of color. Almost all plant dyes fade in sunlight, in washing, or simply as time passes. Only a few substances deliver a dye that is colorfast and lightfast, meaning it will survive direct light

---

31. David, *Fashion Victims*, "A Peculiarly Vivid Green."

and water and not fade through time. Have you heard the phrase "true blue"? That phrase originally referred to a dye from Coventry in England that turned out a blue cloth that wouldn't fade over time.[32]

Natural dyes have deep histories, sometimes glamorous, sometimes dark. Before synthetic dyes, these were among the costliest items to trade—whole empires were built on them. Some of those empires were built on slave labor. The story of red, blue, and bright prints is bound up in the story of the slave trade from India to Africa to the Americas.

We've seen that human bodies respond to the color of light, and that the color of cloth is created from physical dyes based in plants, animals, minerals and metals, or synthetics. You might think that this would make it easy to standardize the meaning of each color. However there is a big jump from the color we see to the meaning of that color. Scientists point out that color is not only about what we see but also what we understand. Physical perception translates into meaning as our eyes report sensation to our brains which in turn interpret what we are seeing.

Our interpretation of color is partially based on our biological reactions, but it is also affected by cultural influence. Color meanings vary from culture to culture. In America brides wear white; in India and many parts of Asia, red is the color of choice, but both colors symbolize purity. In Japan and China purple codes expensive while in America purple registers as cheap.[33] Even the colors we identify vary across cultures. Old Japanese uses one word, *ao*, to

---

32. Taylor, *Coventry*, 8.

33. Marieke de Mooij, *Consumer Behavior and Culture*, 231.

describe both blue and green.[34] And in Japan, green traffic lights can actually be blue!

Each one of us has individual experiences that create our personal associations with color. Your mother refused to let you buy a pink dress because it didn't match your red hair, so now you wear pink frequently to declare your independence. On the other hand, your best friend was forced to wear pink dresses as a girl when she really wanted to climb trees in blue jeans, so for her, pink means oppression. Culturally, pink can mean playfulness—we say we are "tickled pink"!

The color we surround ourselves with can change our mood. The colors we wear express something about us and also what we want to attract. Since it is so physical and also so emotional, the color we choose is one of the most important factors in determining the kind of magic our cords will carry.

To better understand how we can work with color, we can take a quick look at the ways we see colors and how they interact.

Color Wheels

The manner in which we see color, paint color, and how it is rendered on a computer screen are all different processes.

Seeing Color

What happens when ordinary colorless sunlight reaches our eyes? Our eyes have structures called "cones" in them that detect colors. Of these cones, there are actually three types: one for red, one for blue, and one for green.

---

34. Yamada, *The 7 Keys to Communicating in Japan*, 177.

So how do we see all the other colors? Each cone can actually detect a bit of the other colors, and they can work together. The red and green cones working together can see yellow.

Most humans are called "trichromats" because we can see all three colors. Some of us are color blind and have trouble seeing one of the colors.[35] That color is usually green, although sometimes it's red or blue.

A few rare people have one additional cone.[36] This occurs only in people with two x chromosomes, including women and intersex people. Tetrachromats see hundreds more colors than trichromats. We can glimpse the four-cone world in the work of artist Concetta Antico who paints with riotous swirls of color.[37] "Color is power," she says.

So how can you know you are seeing the color other people are seeing? The short answer is that you can't. Have you ever gotten into a color fight with someone? "See that orange over there?" "Orange? That's pink!" In cord magic, what matters is that when you pick a color you know what it means to you.

Painting Color

It's a bit of a surprise to learn that our eyes are configured to notice red, blue, and green—we learned in school that the primary colors are red, yellow, and blue. Painters have long known that mixing these together creates the secondary colors of the rainbow spectrum. Here's a quick reference.

---

35. Colour Blind Awareness, "Types of Colour Blindness."

36. Ossola, "This Woman Sees 100 Times More Colors Than The Average Person."

37. Antico, "Tetrachromancy."

Quick reference
PRIMARY AND SECONDARY COLORS

Colors	Result
Red and yellow	Orange
Red and blue	Purple
Yellow and blue	Green
Red, yellow, and blue	Brown

When I was a kid playing with watercolors, I was so surprised when the bright primary colors all mixed together turned into a muddy brown! This observation is important to cord magic because when you twist colored threads together you may get a result that looks like their mixture—red and blue threads mixed tightly together may look like purple. You can mitigate this effect by adding a neutral strand.

Tip: Adding threads of a neutral color, such as white or black helps other colors in a cord stand out.

There's another color wheel that has more combinations of colors. At the beginning of the twentieth century, Albert Munsell expanded the basic color wheel into ten colors.[38]

---

38. Munsell, "The Munsell Color Wheel Charts & The Theory Behind Them."

Quick Reference
MUNSELL COLOR WHEEL

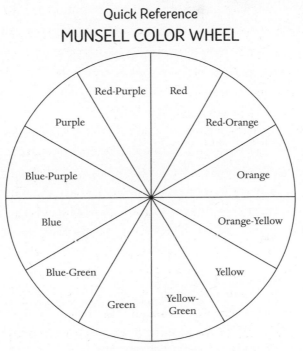

Munsell color wheel

Electronic Display and Printing

If you have ever ordered clothing online or through a catalog, you know that the color you picked may not be the color you get. The way color displays on the computer screen or on the printed page is different from the way it looks to our physical eyes in sunlight. Here's a brief look at why.

Electronic screens paint with light. Our computers, televisions, and monitors use red, green, and blue to create all the other colors in the images. These colors are all assigned a number that tells a web page which color to display. These numbers specify how much red, green, and blue should be displayed to make up the color.

There are two systems that specify the number. The first is "RGB" or red, green, blue. RGB numbers (sometimes called RGB values) specify the percentage of these respective to display. The RGB number for the color yellow is R 255, G 255, B0. The other system is called hexadecimal or hex number. The hex number for yellow is #FFFF00. For white, it is #FFFFFF.

There are many web charts that list the RGB and hex numbers of colors—you don't have to calculate them yourself! There are numerous conversion charts online that translate RGB to hex numbers. The Munsell website (www.munsell.com) has many charts and blog posts that discuss the systems and their conversions.

Printers paint with ink. They use the colors cyan, magenta, and yellow. Each of these overlaps two primary colors. Cyan, yellow, and magenta form black, but it's a pretty muddy black, so printers typically add a fourth well of black ink. This is marked K instead of B to prevent confusion with blue. This also allows for printing black text without the use of the other colors. So the printing color scheme is CMYK.[39]

Quick Reference
PRINTER COLORS

C	Cyan	blue and green
M	Magenta	blue and red
Y	Yellow	green and red
K	Black	black

---

39. Replica Printing, "Why Do Printers Use CMYK?"

Here is the CMYK code that tells the printer to print yellow:

C	M	Y	K
0%	0%	100%	0%

The printing company Pantone set out to standardize color descriptions so that printed colors could be reliably reproduced. The Pantone color system has grown to encompass paint and fabric as well. All the Pantone colors are described in RGB, hex, and CMYK systems. They've become one of the leading authorities on color names and how color is used and reproduced.

What does this mean in choosing colors for cord projects? Over time, we get to know our suppliers. If you are ordering embroidery floss or yarn online, the company almost always numbers their colors, so you can reliably reorder the one you want. Ordering artisan yarns is a little trickier since natural dyes can vary so widely from batch to batch. In this case, the variation is part of the charm!

The Magical Color Palette

The magical color palette comes in the rainbow shades: red, yellow, orange, green, blue, and violet or purple.

Here's a note on the color terms used in this book. In school you may have learned that the rainbow has seven colors. The one missing from the list above is indigo. Isaac Newton saw these colors when he used a prism to separate sunlight into the spectrum. He wanted to add one more color to make up the magic number of seven (for the seven planets and seven musical notes), so he located a shade between blue and violet and added it to his spectrum. He chose the word "indigo" to describe this color, after the indigo plant that gives a deep blue color (a dye with a rich history and meaning all its own). In this book, we discuss indigo with the color blue.

What's the difference between violet and purple? Newton used the word "violet" rather than "purple." Today, violet is generally used to describe a color on the light spectrum. Interior designers study violet along with the colors red, orange, yellow, green, and blue. However, painters and fashion designers refer to "purple" rather than "violet." In pigments and dyes, purple is a secondary color resulting from a one-to-one combination of red and blue. Because cord magic is related to fabric, this book generally uses the term "purple" rather than "violet."

There are so many shades of color, it would be impossible to list them all here. Each of the colors below is really a family of colors. We'll review them briefly in general terms. And in the following section, we'll look at some natural dye substances and how they contribute to the cultural meaning of color.

Red

Red is the color of life. It naturally pops—it doesn't take a lot of the color to attract attention. A red dot on a gray canvas immediately draws the eye. Wherever we see red, we focus on it. That's why traffic signs use red to mean "Stop!"

In the natural world, we are surrounded by the green of plants and the blue of the sky. Red stands out against these backgrounds. Nature uses red to draw our attention to something important.[40] That signal may indicate something dangerous or something helpful—a poisonous red mushroom or a delicious red apple. Many fruits are red, and just saying their names can conjure up their taste: cherry, cranberry, strawberry, raspberry, watermelon, peach.

---

40. Humphrey, "The Colour Currency of Nature."

Red light increases our blood pressure and hormone production. Red is passionate! When we're attracted to someone our heart speeds up. Life and sex, life and love, sex and love are all closely connected. "Roses are red," we say, and we give red flowers to show affection, while a red dress conveys sexy glamour. When we're angry, our eyes are covered with a red haze—we say we are literally "seeing red." When it's associated with red, whatever we feel is sure to be strong.

As we have seen, a single red thread is one of the oldest and most common forms of cord magic. Red is the color of blood: the blood of childbirth, the blood shared by mother and child, the blood that spills when the body is cut. Blood carries the iron in the body, giving it a metallic taste, and we may even faintly taste iron when we see the color blood red.

Red is sex, anger, war, love, blood. While we live, blood circulates in our bodies; if we lose too much blood, we die. Blood is life, and red is the color of life.

Orange

Orange is the color of excitement. Stuck between yellow and red, it shares many of their characteristics. When you read "think of something orange" what's the first thing that comes to your mind? Was it an orange? That's not surprising. The color is named for the fruit—and the word "orange" is shortened from the Persian *narange* and Spanish *naranja*. The word *narange* could have become "arange" in English, but "orange" is more satisfying since it reminds us of the Spanish word *oro*, meaning "gold."[41]

To English, "orange" is a fairly new word. For that reason, orange is the rainbow color with the least synonyms. Another reason is that

---

41. Skeat, *The Concise Dictionary of English Etymology*, 317.

there aren't many things that are naturally orange. Technology has made it possible for us to make glass and paint and fabric in any color we like, so we have orange vases and orange shirts. But where does orange occur in nature? There are a few flowers that are genuinely orange. Poppies, tulips, lilies, and daisies all have vibrant orange varieties. Other flowers listed as orange can also be classified as shades of yellow or red.

The version of the color found most commonly in nature is the low intensity orange, brown.[42] There are lots of words that describe shades of brown, such as "tawny," "amber," and "bronze," to name a few. We can taste brown in cinnamon, cocoa, coffee, and chestnut. Light brown shades to beige and tan.

If orange has a season, it's fall. Leaves turn shades of red, yellow, and brown in autumn. Wheat ripens from green to gold.

Orange is red's less flamboyant cousin. Like red, it is an accent color in nature. It's not as strong as sexy and passionate red but still attracts attention. Web designers use orange to highlight buttons and make important words pop. That's why orange is the color of excitement.

Yellow

Yellow is the color of sunlight. Ordinary sunlight is colorless and illuminates the color of whatever object it spotlights. However, our sun is a yellow star that looks yellow in the sky, so sunlight has been associated with gold in magical correspondences for millennia.[43]

A joyful person has a sunny disposition. When the sun comes out after a storm, we know that everything is going to be alright. As we have seen, our bodies need sunlight, and just being in the

---

42. Kastan, *On Color*, 45.

43. Australia National Telescope Facility. "The Colour of Stars."

sun can shift our mood. The happiness of sunlight transfers to the color yellow.

In addition to being joyful, yellow is considered to be lucky by many cultures, probably because of its association with the value of gold.[44] At one time, the value of American currency was backed by stacks of gold bars in a system called the "gold standard."[45] Gold has been traded as a valuable metal throughout history. It's actually possible to obtain threads made from gold, but as you might expect they are quite expensive. Even threads that mimic the shiny metallic color cost more than ordinary yellow thread. These are worth saving if you remake a cord.

Green

Green is the color of the earth. From space, earth's continents appear covered with green. Whole forests of trees, fields of vegetables, prairies of grasses paint the landscape.

You may remember from school that the green in plants comes from chlorophyll. This pigment lets plants use sunlight to convert water and air into sugar to use as energy. In the process, the plant gives off oxygen, which many living creatures use to convert food into energy. Oxygen breathers in turn give off carbon dioxide, which green plants also use in photosynthesis.[46] Animals and plants live in symbiosis, each providing something the other needs.

We know intellectually that humans need plants to survive. Our bodies know it on a non-conscious level too. Taking a walk in the woods, breathing the air, and bathing in the green light soothes and nourishes us. Green heals us.

---

44. Treadwell, *Red Book of Luck*, 93.

45. Elwell, Brief History of the Gold Standard in the United States, "Summary."

46. Silverstein, *Photosynthesis*, 8–9.

Red, orange, and yellow are stimulating colors. Blue and purple are cooling colors. Green is in the middle, mixing the optimism of yellow with the comfort of blue. Green is also the color of prosperity. One reason is that American money is printed on green paper, but the association goes deeper than that. Green is the most common color in the natural world, so it suggests fertility and abundance. It is so strongly associated with nature that we use the word "green" to mean ecologically sound, making green the color of the earth.

Blue

Blue is the color of peace. Blue light calms us physically by decreasing blood pressure. Blue walls surround us with a sense of gentle security.

We can depend on sturdy and workmanlike blue. In fact, the history of blue is the history of work. Medieval European women and men were sharply restricted in the color of clothing they could wear. Purple was reserved for nobility, and cochineal and kermes red were too expensive for normal wear. Peasants were discouraged from wearing gaudy clothing and restricted to dark shades like black and brown. The one spot of color permitted to the non-nobility was blue. It was wildly popular.

Everyone wears blue jeans now, but up until the 1930s denim was the uniform of the working class.[47] The sturdy fabric was first manufactured in Genoa, or Genes, so pants made from this material came to be called "jeans."[48] In 1874 American tailor Jacob Davis developed a sturdy cloth and riveted the seams for durability. He

---

47. Miller, *Global Denim*, 26.

48. Roshan, *Denim*, 194.

teamed up with businessman Levi Strauss to patent the idea. The Levi Strauss company continues to make jeans today.

Blue is the color of the working police force too. In the American Civil War, officers wore red coats but common soldiers wore blue ones. When they retired, they passed their blue coats to the earliest police forces.[49] In England, the first bobbies chose blue for their color because it was cheap and because it was different from the bright red uniforms of the soldiers.

Before synthetic dyes, jeans received their color from indigo. It wasn't just beautiful, the dye made the cloth stronger. Most dyes react chemically to fabric, but indigo bonds physically at the molecular level.[50] A fabric dyed with indigo will not fade in sunlight but will fade with rubbing, giving it that distinct broken-in look associated with physical labor.

The saddest reason that blue is the color of work is because of slavery. When the British colonized India, they moved in to supervise the native production of indigo. Under colonization, formerly independent Indian dyers worked under the watchful eye of the overseers who took the profits from their work. Indigo plants were shipped to the Caribbean to be grown there too. Relatedly, indigo was one of the major drivers of the slave trade.[51] European landowners bought colorful fabrics from India and traded them in Africa with the tribes that kidnapped other Africans to sell to the slavers. These Africans were shipped to the Caribbean to grow indigo on plantations alongside enslaved natives.

---

49. Los Angeles Police Museum, "LAPD's Finest."

50. Kassinger, *Dyes*, 44.

51. Taussig, *What Color Is the Sacred?*, 130–140.

Although the sun in a cloudless sky shines yellow, the sky itself looks blue when we look up at it. Interestingly, the earth's atmosphere also looks blue when we look down at it from the perspective of space.[52] Here's why. Sunlight contains all the rainbow colors. The sunlight hitting the atmosphere is scattered in all directions. The wavelength of blue is shorter than the other scattered colors, so more blue hits our eyes than any other wavelength. Large bodies of water such as lakes and the ocean also look blue. Water absorbs more of the longer wavelength colors such as red and orange, so the wavelength that gets returned to our eyes is blue.[53]

Just as blue light relaxes us, being around water is calming too. Partly it's the effect of the color itself, and it's also because the human race evolved to gravitate to water, which we need almost as much as we need oxygen. It's the color of sky and water that makes blue the color of peace.

Purple

Purple is the color of power. In the palace of the Byzantine empire was a room built entirely of purple rock. The women of the imperial families would retire into this room to give birth so that the heirs to the empire were literally born "in the purple"![54]

Purple was specifically royal because of the staggering expense of purple cloth. In Rome and Byzantium, only the very wealthy could afford the color. Purple dye came from a snail, and it took 10,000 murex shellfish to produce one gram of dye. It was so dif-

---

52. Siegel, "Why Does Earth Appear Blue From Space?"

53. *Scientific American*, "Why does the ocean appear blue?"

54. Paspates, *The Great Palace of Constantinople*, 346.

ficult and time consuming to extract the color from the snails that the dye was more valuable than gold.[55]

As for the snail, it was harvested in the ancient city of Tyre. The inhabitants of Tyre told a charming story to explain how they had discovered the dye. It seems that Hercules was walking along the sea shore with the nymph Tyrus. His dog ran ahead and ate a snail which turned his mouth purple. Tyrus demanded a cloth dyed the same color, so Hercules gathered enough snails to make the cloth for his lady-love.[56]

Tyre exported dyed cloth to the entire Mediterranean world. Ugaritic and Hittite texts from 1400 BCE mention Tyrian purple. The very name of the people who produced the dye, *Phoenician*, derives from the Greek word *phoinios*, purple. By all accounts, Tyrian purple could describe anything from a light red to a very deep red to a color closer to what we think of as purple today, commonly called "maximum purple."

With the creation of synthetic dyes, purple lost its connection to royalty but still carries the association of richness and even spirituality, and remains the color of power.

White and Black

White and black are neutral colors. In the history of color, white, red, and black is one of the oldest color combinations.[57] Adding red to black and white brings in the resonance of all the meanings color has ever had.

There is a cultural meaning to black and white that is the opposite of neutral but is judgmental. In this meaning white is light and

---

55. Cartwright, "Tyrian Purple."

56. Gaboriaud-Kolar, *A Colorful History*, 89.

57. Erica Reiner, *Astral Magic*, 125.

black is shadow; white is good, black is evil. These associations developed in the colonial era to justify slavery by proving the moral superiority of white-skinned people over black-skinned people.

Isaac Newton demonstrated that when sunlight shines through a prism, it separates into the colors of the rainbow. Before light is split into the spectrum it is colorless. However, Newton didn't call this light colorless—he called it white. Newton's friend Robert Boyle was one of the founders of the earliest scientific organization, The Royal Society of London. He was also a director of the East India Company, which was heavily involved in the slave trade. These two interests came together in Boyle's experiments with light. He decided that white objects reflect light while black objects "deaden" light. White is the original pure color and black discolors white. Boyle applied these findings to explain why white-skinned European people possess reason whereas black people were clearly marked to be their servants. Newton accepted his description of light as "white," and science has called light "white" ever since.[58]

To be clear, "white light" is a racist term, as is "black magic." The latter refers specifically to the medicine and spirituality practiced by dark-skinned slaves and their descendants. For this reason, this book explicitly rejects the association of good and evil with white and black.

While daylight is generally positive and night generally recognized as dangerous, other cultures see the colors black and white differently. In America, white is the color of weddings and black is the color of funerals, but in many cultures of Africa and Asia, white has historically been the color of death, although this is changing with the influence of European-American culture on the world.[59]

---

58. Williams, *White Light, Black Magic*, "The Scientist."
59. Reis, *Death is a Festival*, 96. See also Hibi, *The Colors of Japan*, 6.

We can look to interior design for the emerging meaning of white and black. White and black can be paired with any of the colors of the rainbow. In fact, it's a good idea to include either white or black in cords to prevent the colors from mixing; for example, red and blue mixed together register as purple to the eye. Black and white therefore provide contrast without bringing in color of their own, making them both neutral.

Planetary colors

In magic, the elements and planets also have colors. It's pretty easy to figure out where the elemental colors come from because they physically look like their colors. The air is yellow with sunlight, water reflecting the sky is blue, fire is orange and red, and the plants of the earth surround us with green. But why do the planets have color?

First are the magical planets. The first Babylonian astrologers counted any object that moved in the sky as a planet, so they added the sun and moon to the other visible planets. That's how we came to have seven "planets" in the magical association list. Today's astronomical tools can see much farther than the human eye, so the outer planets—Neptune, Uranus, and Pluto—were added to the list. Then astronomers started to debate which objects deserve to be called planets and excluded Pluto. Some astrologers today include Neptune and Pluto with the classic list of planets.

The magical planets came to their current color associations first through their physical color, then the color associated with the planet by the ancient peoples who built planetary temples, and later the esoteric association of the planets with the colors of the spectrum.

The planets have a physical color when observed with the naked eye. The Babylonians observed the planets in clear desert skies. They built temples called ziggurats which look like pyramids with steps and associated the steps of the temples with the colors of the planets.[60] Astrologer Rumen Kolev gives Babylonian color correspondences for the planets: Venus, white; Saturn, gray; Mars, red; moon, blue; Jupiter, orange; Mercury, variable; sun, yellow.[61]

Alchemists, astrologers, and occultists have long attempted to map the seven planets known to the ancients to rainbow colors while taking the physical appearance of the planets into account. The colors associated with the planets in the Western Magical Tradition today were set by the Hermetic Order of the Golden Dawn. Chief Adept Florence Farr worked with the colors of the spectrum. Richard Dudschus and David Sledzinski created a list from Farr's notes: moon, blue; Mercury, yellow; Venus, emerald green; Sun, orange; Mars, scarlet; Jupiter, violet; Saturn, indigo.[62]

When Aleister Crowley compiled his *Encyclopedia 777*, he changed a few of the associations. Because of the popularity of *777*, these have become common in magical work today: moon, violet; Mercury, orange; Venus, emerald; Sun, yellow; Mars, red; Jupiter, blue; Saturn, black.[63] In this book, we work with Crowley's planetary colors as our reference.

---

60. Handcock, *Mesopotamian Archaeology*, 143.

61. Kolev, "Some Reflections about Babylonian Astrology."

62. Dudschus, *Coloring the Classic Golden Dawn Tarot.*

63. Crowley, *777*, 71.

Quick reference
PLANETARY COLORS

Planet	Color
Moon	White, silver, or lavender
Mercury	Orange
Venus	Green
Sun	Yellow
Mars	Red
Jupiter	Blue
Saturn	Black

Dyes

We've said before that dye is the body of color. Before synthetic colors were developed in 1857, pigments and dyes came from specific physical sources—rocks, plants, insects, earth. Painters still use these, their names an evocative memory of a past age. There are the earths, raw and burnt sienna, raw and burnt umber, golden ochre. All the reds: madder lake, vermilion, venetian red. There's indigo, which comes from plants, and ultramarine, originally from ground up lapis lazuli. Some of these substances are still used as dyes, not commercially but in small batches used by indigenous peoples and fiber artists.

The history of these dyes contributes to the cultural meaning of the color. In many cases, the color of the substance matches the color of the dye. Cochineal insects are bright red and turmeric is very yellow. In other cases, the dye color only shows up in the end—indigo changes from orange to green to blue.

Here is a look at some of the natural substances used to dye fabric.

The Natural Dye Palette

Red Dyes

Carmine, vermilion, cardinal red—these colors all refer to physical substances. Before the invention of synthetic dyes, we got our red dye from a plant and from an insect.[64]

Madder from the plant *Rubia tinctoria* has been traded as a colorfast dye and a medicine since the third millennium BCE. It flourishes all over Europe, Asia, and Africa, and is so easy to grow that weavers still grow it in the home garden today. Madder's red pigment is called alizarin, yielding the alizarin crimson of the artist's palette.

Madder gives a bright red, but there's an even brighter natural shade. The Mediterranean insect *Kermes vermilio* gives us the words "crimson" and "vermilion," "crimson" from the Turkish *kirmiz* and vermilion from the Latin *vermiculus*, itself a diminutive of *vermis*, or "worm." Kermes dye yields a brighter red than madder, but the effort to gather the insects and produce the dye has always made it considerably more expensive than madder.

Kermes crimson was the brightest red available until a New World discovery knocked it from its top spot. The carmine dye derived from the cochineal insect yields both crimson (a bluish red) and scarlet (a yellowish red).[65] We still use cochineal today as a food coloring, leading to periodic breathless blog posts with titles such as "The red in food comes from BUGS!"

---

64. Kassinger, *Dyes: From Sea Snails to Synthetics*, 47–56.

65. Hummel, *The Dyeing of Textile Fabrics*, 275.

Both vermilion and madder dyes express military and national power. The Spanish empire grew wealthy from the cochineal dye produced on New World plantations by the labor of enslaved people. British soldiers were called "redcoats" for their uniforms; they were dyed with madder for infantry and cochineal for officers.[66] The red in early American flags derives from madder or a combination of madder and cochineal.[67]

Red dyes also express religious power. Catholic cardinals wear hats dyed scarlet, specifically the color derived from the cochineal insect, which is why it also came to be known as cardinal red.

Today these dyes are artisan products. If you want to dive first-hand into the history of color, you can grow your own madder from seed to make your own dye. Both madder and cochineal dyes are available in small craft lots. You can also find skeins of wool yarn hand-dyed with madder and cochineal.

Orange Dyes

In dyes as in the light spectrum, orange lies between red and yellow. We've talked about madder dye under red but madder can produce a range of colors depending on the mordant (dye fixative) used. The range varies from deep red through vibrant orange to muted pink. One of those colors is the khaki brown used for uniforms, including the trousers worn by corporate workers! Many of the dyes that result in yellow can also shade toward orange or gold.

Where orange comes into its own is in shades of brown. Tree barks and nuts produce shades of brown. The Indian dye cutch brown comes from the bark of the acacia tree. American black walnut produces a deep brown tincture settlers used to dye clothing

66. Orr, *The New American Herbal*, 231.

67. Holm, "Why these colors don't run."

and to color hair.[68] For an easy dye to make in your own kitchen, brown onion skins give various shades of beige to dark brown.

Yellow Dyes

Generally speaking, plants that look yellow make yellow dyes. Have you ever cooked with turmeric? Did you notice how it can stain your countertop? It also stains cloth and was used as a commercial dye for centuries. The saffron spice gathered from crocus flowers also makes a yellowish dye, as do flowers such as goldenrod, marigold, Queen Anne's lace, and dyer's broom.[69]

Plant-based dyes can be beautiful but tend to fade in sunlight. There is one plant that gives a lightfast yellow dye: weld, *Reseda luteola*. The Romans used the plant to dye both wedding robes and the robes of the Vestal virgins.[70] Like madder, weld can be grown in the home garden for hand-dyeing fibers. Artisan dyers offer beautiful wool skeins dyed weld.

Green Dyes

Interestingly, while green is the most common color in nature, it is very difficult to find a substance that will create a green dye, which is why the arsenic-based dye Scheele's green was so popular even though it was dangerous.[71] Medieval European dyers leveraged the fact that yellow and blue make green to create green dye, using a combination of woad for blue and weld for yellow. Woad and weld create the Lincoln green that Robin Hood wore in the

---

68. Liles, *The Art and Craft of Natural Dyeing*, 174.

69. Liles, *The Art and Craft of Natural Dyeing*, 33–34.

70. Brunello, *The Art of Dyeing in the History of Mankind*, 107.

71. Jennifer Wright, "The History of Green Dye."

forest. And after the introduction of indigo, dyers combined that blue with yellow dyes to create green.

Blue Dyes

In Europe, the earliest blue came from the woad plant. Julius Caesar said "all the Britons dye themselves with woad, which produces a blue colour."[72] The woad trade supported entire towns; dried woad plants were crushed and packed into balls that could be shipped easily.[73]

Woad gives a lovely blue color, but indigo is outstanding. Indigo is a *pharmakon*. This is a complicated word, one of the many Greek words translated as "magic." It can refer to a charm, a spell, a medicine, a potion or poison, a paint or a dye. *Indikos pharmakon* is the magical substance that came from India.[74] As far back as the eighth century, Europe traded with India for the dye. The costly import was substantially more expensive than homegrown woad, and it eventually sparked the trade in slaves who produced both plants and dyes for European profiteers.

Interestingly, it's relatively easy to find artisan fabric and yarn dyed with indigo, but harder today to find woad-dyed wool.

Purple Dyes

The snail that gave Tyrian purple is endangered and there is no longer a Mediterranean dye industry.[75] However, purple mollusks all over the world give a purple color. Since pre-Conquest times,

---

72. Deming, *Science and Technology in World History, Volume 4*, 19.

73. Thompson, *The Materials and Techniques of Medieval Painting*, 137.

74. Liddell, "Pharmakon."

75. Beaumont, "Ancient shellfish used for purple dye vanishes from eastern Med."

Mixtec people have used the *Purpura patula* snail to create a purple dye called *tixinda*. Artisans in the natural crafts business have made treks to remote Oaxacan villages to watch Mixtec women and men dye, spin, and weave the native cotton.[76]

Because purple is so close to red, madder dye has been used to create purplish shades. Artisans who experiment with natural shades use red cabbage to create a non-colorfast purplish shade.

White and Black Dyes

In its darkest range, indigo dye can approach the color black. Medieval European dyers used a combination of the primary dye colors to produce black, mixing indigo and madder with a yellow dye such as weld.[77]

Cotton and flax fibers make cloth that bleaches in the sun, so there hasn't been a real need to develop a white dye. Wool naturally occurs in both white and black shades. If you're using wool yarn with natural colors for your magic, you don't actually need a white or black dye at all.

Growing Your Own Dye Plants

The primary pigments are red, yellow, and blue. You can grow the three primary colorfast and lightfast dye plants—madder, weld, and woad—in your own garden. I love having a few individual plants for their history and energy. However, it takes quite a few plants to make a usable dye, and learning how to extract the dye is a commitment to learning a craft. If this calls to you, I encourage you to explore Rita Buchanan's *A Weaver's Garden*. Her book gives

---

76. Geri Anderson, "Looms, weavers and the sacred snail on Mexico's Costa Chica."

77. Liles, *Art and Craft of Natural Dyeing*, 184.

instructions for growing plants and extracting dyes. She also details a simple method of extracting coloring agents from plants in a simple dye-bath using hot water.

Madder dye is made from the roots. The plant is a perennial, hardy to -5 degrees Fahrenheit, so it can grow outdoors up to zone 6, but you'll need to kill the plant to harvest the roots, and it takes between two and five years to grow the plant to a sufficient size to have a usable amount of roots. You can buy seeds if you want to have the plant in your garden. You can also buy the roots directly if you want to dive into the dye-making art.

Weld, or dyer's rocket, takes two years to grow. It makes plenty of seeds which can be collected to grow more plants. Woad also takes two years to mature and its seeds scatter so easily that it can become invasive—be sure to contain your plants! Dye is made from the leaves of both plants, which can be harvested as the plant grows, or all at once. However it takes quite a few plants to harvest enough leaves to make a usable amount.

Using Natural Dyes

If you have the time and inclination, working with natural dyes is a great way to put yourself in touch with the physical sources of color. They're also beautiful! You can buy undyed wool to color yourself. Online marketplaces sell natural dyes such as cochineal and indigo, although these are a bit complicated to use; you'll want to study how to use them. Fiber guilds offer classes and can put you in touch with experienced people to help you learn.

You can also create your own dyes with vegetables and spices. These dyes are easy to make in your home kitchen.[78] Vegetable

---

78. Martha Stewart, "Natural Dyes from Plants and Vegetables." See also Mali Anderson, "How to Make Natural Dyes from Fruits and Vegetables."

dyes are easier to use than the cochineal and indigo, although they may wash out in water or light. Dyeing your own yarn adds a lot of power to the cord.

Quick Reference
NATURAL DYE MATERIALS[79]

Color	Plant
Red	Madder, cochineal, beets
Orange	Madder
Brown	Black walnut, onion skins
Beige	Goldenrod
Yellow	Broom, weld, saffron, turmeric
Blue	Indigo, woad
Green	A yellow and a green dye, for example indigo and weld, or cabbage and turmeric
Purple	Red cabbage, blueberries, blackberries, elderberries

You can make dyes in your kitchen with common vegetables. Here are the most common and easiest to try:

• **Red:** beets

• **Orange, yellow, brown:** onion skins, turmeric

• **Blue, purple:** red cabbage, blueberries

---

79. See Buchanan, *A Weaver's Garden* and Liles, *The Art and Craft of Natural Dyeing* for detail and recipes.

- **Green:** dye first with a yellow dye such as turmeric, then soak in a blue dye such as cabbage

Quick Reference
DYE YOUR OWN YARN

1. **Pick the fabric.** Use a natural fabric or undyed yarn. You can use cotton or linen bags or cord, but wool picks up color most easily. You can find undyed wool yarn online through natural dye and fabric suppliers.

2. **Make the dye water.** For vegetables: chop the vegetable. Cover with twice as much water as vegetable. Bring this to boil and then simmer for an hour. Strain out the vegetable (eat if you want!) Let the dye water cool. For turmeric: use 2 teaspoons of turmeric to 2 cups of water.

3. **Treat the fiber.** You will need to treat the fabric or yarn before you can dye it by boiling it in 1 part vinegar to 4 parts water. Bring the water to a boil, then simmer the yarn or cloth in the water for one hour. Dry it completely.

4. **Dye the fiber.** Soak the yarn or cloth in the dye for 12 hours or so. Overnight works well.

5. **Rinse the fiber.** Soak the fiber in a bowl of clean water and then wring it out. This will help get some of the vinegar and vegetable smell out of the fiber.

6. **Dry the fiber.** Hanging the fiber on a line outside to dry airs out the fiber and also helps to disperse the vegetable and vinegar scent.

These dyes aren't colorfast or lightfast—they will fade in sunlight and water. They're somewhat disappointing to use in projects such as T-shirts that need to be laundered because the dyes will wash out. However, they work well in a project with a cord that hopefully won't need washing. The shades from vegetable dyes are muted but have a natural beauty. It's especially thrilling to dip turmeric-dyed fiber into the cabbage dye and come up with green.

You can make vegetable dyes in the kitchen with cooking pans and bowls. Working with madder, cochineal, weld, and indigo requires using alum as a mordant which will need a dedicated pot. To explore this dye method, my fiber friends recommend the Buchanan book mentioned earlier and Michele Wipplinger's *Natural Dye Instruction Booklet*.

Synthetic Dyes

If you're not using yarn dyed with a natural substance, you're using a synthetic dye. Synthetic dyes give a great range of color choices and work perfectly well in cord magic. After all, the most important thing in working with colored yarn is that you are happy with the color. Today, synthetic dyes come in every imaginable shade of color and can be reproduced reliably.

The very first synthetic dye hit the market as a substitute for Tyrian purple. William Henry Perkin was a whiz kid.[80] At fifteen, he was already enrolled in the Royal College studying chemistry. And in 1856, when he was just eighteen, he spent Easter break in his laboratory experimenting with coal tar trying to synthesize quinine. He didn't get it, but what he did discover instead revolutionized dyes forever.

---

80. Long, "How Mauve Was Her Garment."

Perkin noticed that one of the substances he synthesized left a purple sludge on his lab equipment. He stuck a bit of silk in the sludge and came up with a brilliant purple. Further experimenting proved it was colorfast and lightfast—it didn't fade in sunlight or wash out in the laundry. Perkin abandoned his mentor and his college chemistry studies, obtained a loan from his father, and founded a factory to produce the dye commercially. He called it "Tyrian purple," later renamed "mauveine" after the French word for a purplish flower.

Royalty went mad for mauveine. The French Empress Eugenie liked the way it matched her eyes. When Queen Victoria turned up at the Royal Exhibition of 1862 wearing a mauveine-dyed silk dress, Perkin's success was assured.

Mauveine was the first of the aniline dyes derived from coal tar, and the race was on to bring out new shades. These were so inexpensive to make and so attractive to use that the commercial natural dye industry died out completely in just a few years.

Unfortunately, coal tar-based dyes and the success of its industry has come at a cost to the environment. Aniline or azo dyes are used in such quantities that industrial contamination is a serious problem. In "Toxic Threads," Greenpeace notes that these dyes give off cancer-causing byproducts. Denim jean factories in the heartland of Mexico use the same rivers that irrigate the corn fields and the dyes used in manufacturing the jeans dye the rivers blue.[81] Greenpeace calls on manufacturers to commit to eliminating toxic byproducts, on governments to require them to do so, and on consumers to demand that both manufacturers and governments step up to address this issue.[82]

---

81. Daniel, "Jeans firms pollute Mexican city with blue dye."
82. Greenpeace, "Toxic Threads."

We've looked at the colors of nature, the color of light, the history of dyes, and the color of the planets. This is a good time to revisit the worksheet "My Color Meanings" on page 68. Do you have new ideas to add to your color associations?

Cord magic is fiber magic. Our next design step is to decide which fabric we will use to create our cords.

six
Fiber

Cords make magic tangible. A cord is a talisman made from a string. The fiber of the string is the body of the talisman. The physical material adds both practical and energetic qualities to our magical intent.

Fiber is a call to kinship with the living things of the world. Wool yarn begins life in a barn or in the mountains or on the open plain. Cotton, linen, bamboo, and hemp yarns begin life as plants. Synthetic fiber goes through many processing steps but also starts out as plant material. We will review the background of each of these materials to explore what they can bring to our magic and how we can use each of these fibers ethically.

We already have personal associations with fabrics just as we have with color. We've been wearing clothes all our lives so we already know what fabrics we like against our skin and what we avoid. Today's clothing is mostly made from mixtures of natural and synthetic materials, as are our sheets and blankets. Purses, belts, and shoes are made from leather, cotton, canvas, nylon, and polyester. We use these same materials in cord magic. Whether you are new to fiber crafts or very experienced, cord magic offers us a chance to explore the world of fabric. Before we dive into the background of how fabric is made, take a moment to record the meaning of each fabric to you based on your personal preferences. You can note that you wear it, you don't wear it, you have an ethical objection to wearing it, you like the way it looks or feels.

Leather is included here because it's a material used in cords that is worn against the skin. That said, real leather isn't a fabric, as it's made from animal hide. Artificial leather is made from polyester and other synthetics.

Worksheet
MY FIBER MEANINGS

Fiber	Meaning
Bamboo	
Cotton	
Leather	
Linen (flax and hemp)	
Rayon	
Silk	

Fiber	Meaning
Synthetic (acrylic, nylon, polyester)	
Wool	

The fibers in our lives are grown or manufactured, then processed, and finally made into items we use. The meaning of the fiber comes from its original source and from how we interact with it—not only how it looks and feels, but how expensive it is and our ethical stance about how it is created.

Quick Reference
FIBER MEANINGS

Fiber	Meaning
Bamboo	Plant, quick-growing plant, versatile
Cotton	Plant, widely available, gentle on skin
Leather	A non-fabric material. Animal, requires killing the animal, durable and protective. Artificial leather is made from synthetic materials.
Linen	Plant, difficult to process and care for, beautiful look and drape
Rayon	Manufactured from plant material, substitute for silk
Synthetic	Acrylic, nylon and polyester, created from oil, inexpensive and versatile, can irritate skin

Fiber	Meaning
Silk	Insect, mostly requires killing the insect, beautiful and cooling, expensive
Wool	Animal, does not require killing the animal, beautiful and warming, can irritate skin

Any of these materials can be found as threads, yarns, or strings to create cords.

The History of Fabric

One of the most interesting things about cord magic is how old it is. It also connects us to the energies of plants and animals. The way we create fabric is the history of our relationship to the natural world. It is specifically the story of how our species has changed and shaped the natural world. Our earliest ancestors gathered plants and killed and ate animals while walking naked. When we started wearing clothing ourselves, we initiated a whole new way of relating to animals and plants.

Hunting and Gathering

Humans learned to make string at the dawn of our history as a species. In hunter-gatherer societies, women live together to raise children while men band together to hunt.[83] That was true for most humans early in our history and is still true for some people today. Raising children means feeding them and giving them clothing. Gathering means collecting plants. Hunting can mean killing large animals as well as capturing small animals in nets.

---

83. Bertonis, *Stone Age Divas*, 40.

With plant string and leather strips, we could make nets to catch fish and game, tie spear heads to shafts, and create pouches to carry food.[84] Plant fibers spun into thread can be woven into cloth. Spinning, net making, knitting, and weaving are human activities—any gender can do them. However, they are difficult to do while moving rapidly as hunting bands do but easier to do in settlements raising children. Researchers are re-evaluating the stories about "man the hunter" to give more of the spotlight to "woman the innovator"! Women have been spinning thread and weaving cloth since the Paleolithic era and continue to do so today.

Paleolithic Europeans made skirts made of strings dangling from a waist cord. What were they for? Carrying objects, attracting attention, magic? Sometimes the strings were capped with metal, including gold. Only women wore these, and from the quality of the metal and the elaborately carved figurines, it seems they were marked as the highest status people. Most interestingly, they wore the string skirts behind, over their buttocks! It must have been captivating to watch the strings swish as the women walked.[85]

Domesticating Animals

Domesticating animals brought a whole new dimension to the human-animal relationship. Today, humans have responsibilities to care for the animals in exchange for their gifts of milk, meat, and leather. Tending animals binds us to their magic as well as to the magic of the land that nourishes them.

In the Paleolithic era, when a large animal was killed, people could simply camp near the animal until it was consumed. After settlements developed in the Neolithic age, butchered meat could

---

84. Soffer, "The 'Venus' Figurines."

85. Bertonis, *Stone Age Divas*, 104.

be hauled home. Smaller animals could also be brought back to the camp and penned up as a banked food supply. In the springtime the more docile of the animals would quietly reproduce. Over time the animals we domesticated developed characteristics of younger animals. They look like babies and we respond to them in some of the ways we do to human babies.

Permanent settlements made fabric innovations possible. Nomadic women used band or back strap looms that could be tied around the waist with the other end tied to an object such as a tree. Looms like this are still in use among women of some tribes. Staying in one place allowed for the development of larger looms that could weave wider bands of cloth. The ends of the warp were staked to the ground or weighted with clay and stone. These looms develop into larger table and floor looms, tools still in use among traditional artisans in many places in the world today.[86]

Mass Production

The next big step in our relationship to the natural world was industrialization. Today it's hard to imagine how important clothing was before the invention of the industrial loom. A single garment took many hours of hand labor to produce. Only the very richest people worldwide owned more than a few changes of clothing.

The industrial revolution was partly driven by the need for cloth. One of the first mass-production machines was the Jacquard loom which replaced human labor with automated cloth production.[87] Jacquard looms are also still in use today in traditional communities; I personally saw one in use in Varansi in a weaving factory.

---

86. Barber, *Women's Work*, 81.

87. Geselowitz, "The Jacquard Loom."

Before the industrial revolution, the house was the center of productivity. Food came from the garden and backyard livestock. Women and men wove cloth, knitted, and created household items from clay and wood. After the industrial revolution men, women, and even children left home to work in factories. The home changed from a place of production to a place of consumption where the family consumes cloth and food made elsewhere through mass production.

This is the context in which we make our magic today. We use materials which reach us as fully finished end products. Studying how these materials are made brings us back into touch with our human past and the sources of our magic.

What Fabric is Made From

Fiber is made from plants and animals. The cultivation of linen, wool, silk, and cotton developed before the invention of writing. They've been built into human culture for many thousands of years and connect us to the roots of our magic. Some magical folk will only use these fabrics in magical cords or robes.

Today, fabric is also manufactured from plant material and from oil. These materials are still physical although they carry the energy of being processed. While the older fibers carry more of the natural energy, the newer fibers have the advantage of being inexpensive and easy to work with.

Plant Fibers

Cotton

Cotton grows in fluffy bolls on a commercially grown plant. When made into cloth, it's light, soft against the skin, and cool. It's breathable, which means it lets air against the skin, and it's non-allergenic, so it's a very popular clothing fabric. It can be made into a number of textures, including flannel, velvet, velour, corduroy, chambray, and jersey.

Cotton yarn is used by handcrafters to make cotton clothing and utilitarian objects such as towels and place mats. It's not as springy as wool or synthetic thread; it makes a stiffer fabric than the other two. However, it is the most popular material used in embroidery thread and is very often used in cord magic.

Ethical considerations: All industrial fabric production has an environmental impact and sometimes involves human rights violations. Cotton is grown commercially with pesticides and uses up a tremendous amount of water. Processing cotton also involves the use of heavy chemicals.[88] Another concern with cotton is the treatment of the people who produce it. In the United States, cotton historically was grown and processed by black slaves. Even today, cotton from forced labor farms in Uzbekistan makes its way into the global cotton market.[89]

Linen

Linen is a fabric woven from plant fibers, usually flax or hemp. Linen is one of our earliest fabrics. One early example from Catal Huyuk is 9,000 years old![90] Egyptian commoners, royalty, and temple staff all wore flax linen, wrapped mummies in it, and dressed living deity statues in the cloth.[91] Mesopotamian priests and priest-

---

88. Soil Association, "Thirsty for fashion?"

89. Bilal, *Cotton Cultivation*, 33.

90. Hurriyet Daily News, "Centuries-old fabric found in Catalhoyuk."

91. Christina Riggs, *Unwrapping Ancient Egypt*, 1.

esses could have worn wool but chose to wear linen and to wrap the statues of their living goddesses and gods in the fabric.

Linen made from hemp has been used in China for at least two thousand years. In ancient China, those who couldn't afford silk wore clothing made of hemp. This versatile plant also provided paper and rope.

Both flax and hemp linen are widely available today as cloth and thread.

Animal and Insect Fibers

Leather

Put simply, leather is the hide or skin of any animal, wild or domestic. It's not a fabric or fiber per se, but it is a material that we use in some of the same ways as fabric. Skins can be used in large sheets, sinews are made into thread. Commercially available cordage includes leather made from cows, but also includes other animals such as goats, deer and even snake.

Ethical considerations: using leather requires killing the animal. Vegetarians, vegans, and animal rights activists often avoid the use of leather products.

Wool

Wool is one of the basic fibers of the world. Mesopotamian people wore wool as their primary fabric, and traditional cultures around the world still wear wool garments wherever sheep, goats, and camels are raised.[92]

Sheep wool and goat hair make the yarns most widely available commercially, but virtually any animal fur or hair can be spun into

---

92. Mehta-Jones, *Life in Ancient Mesopotamia*, 14.

thread. My yarn stash includes llama and camel yarn. Today, people even collect the hair from their cats and dogs and spin it into thread!

People who work with fiber call the feel of a cloth its "hand." Wool has a wonderful, soft hand. Wool is durable and keeps the wearer warm even when wet, which makes wool socks essential hiking gear. It comes in the color of sheep—white, brown, grey, and black—but it dyes well and can be found in every imaginable color. Wool has a reputation for being scratchy, but good quality wool processed properly can be very soft and comfortable. The breed of sheep called Merino makes a wool that is particularly prized for being soft and light. Merino wool socks are wildly comfortable.

When wool gets wet, it mats in a process known as felting. Felted wool is durable and water resistant. Knitters can turn wool hats into felt hats by hand or by putting them into a washing machine, then placing the hat over a bowl while it dries. Felting shrinks the finished product, so you'll need to take that into account. The felting quality of wool means that finished pieces such as hats, scarves, and blankets can't be machine washed; they must instead be hand washed and carefully dried.

Sheep wool

The vast majority of the wool sold in yarn skeins comes from sheep. The sheep are sheared of their wool once or twice a year. The natural fiber comes in white, brown, or black. White wool is dyed with natural and synthetic dyes in all the rainbow shades.

Most commercial wool has been scoured with chemicals to remove lanolin, the oil produced by sheep as a defense against the elements. Some think it's the harsh scouring that makes wool itchy. Lanolin itself is used commercially in moisturizing lotion, soap and shampoo, and waterproofing. If you are allergic to wool, it's likely that lanolin is the culprit.

It is possible to obtain wool yarn which still contains lanolin. This is my favorite wool yarn, it feels great in the hand, and it smells like sheep!

Ethical considerations: sheep are raised commercially for wool in a number of countries. A number of practices affect their health and quality of life, including mutilation, spraying the animals with pesticides, and live transport which results in deaths. Advocates for humane textile production argue against these practices.[93]

Goat wool: Mohair and cashmere

Angora goats make mohair fiber. (Confusingly, there is also a fiber that comes from rabbits also called angora.) Goat mohair acts a lot like wool in that it's durable and easy to dye. Unlike sheep wool, mohair does not conduct heat, so it is cool to wear in the summer. For that reason it is sometimes blended with wool to make summer weight fabrics. You can find yarn of mohair blended with wool in your favorite yarn shop or online store.

The other goat fiber is cashmere. Cashmere goats produce two coats, a protective outer layer and a warm and soft inner layer. It takes some time for cashmere goats to produce the hair, and it has to be combed out or sheared by hand, then separated from the outer coat, so cashmere is a rare and expensive fiber. It's valuable because it is one of the softest fibers in the world. Like mohair it is often mixed with wool, or with nylon for durability and stretch.

Ethical considerations: in China cashmere goats are herded in vast numbers across landscapes which turn into desert in their wake.[94] Mongolian cashmere tends to come from smaller family-run farms, so textile producers who source from humane producers

---

93. Compassion in world farming, "Welfare issues for sheep."

94. Schmitz, "How Your Cashmere Sweater Is Decimating Mongolia's Grasslands."

often look there. Traditional herders are working together to address overgrazing issues on public lands.[95]

Rabbit Fiber: Angora

Angora rabbits make an incredibly soft fluffy hair. It's sheared like sheep so the Angora rabbit is considered a no-kill livestock.[96] Like mohair and cashmere, angora is warm and beautiful. Unlike other animal fibers it's difficult to spin, so it's often spun into thread with wool.

It's easy to mix up mohair, cashmere, and angora because they are all warm, soft, and often blended with wool. They are similar in terms of the way they feel in the hand. They do come from very different animals which may be important to your magic. If your magic steers you away from any of these animals, or from animal products in general, it's good to know what to avoid. If you love sheep as I do you will love working with wool; if you have an affinity for goats, mohair and cashmere may be attractive; if you work with rabbits, you may be attracted to angora.

Ethical considerations: the vast majority of angora wool comes from China where husbandry practices cause considerable pain to the animals. When these practices came to light a few years ago, a number of retailers dropped angora altogether. They turned away from cashmere and mohair and toward alpaca wool. This has had the positive effect of generating an industry for small Peruvian farmers. This industry remains in the hands of native and small farmers who use sustainable practices.[97]

---

95. Ferry, "Pasture degradation".

96. McLaughlin, *Hobby Farms*, 31.

97. Purdy, "Review of the July 2017 Nunoa Project Veterinary Work in Peru August 2017."

Alpaca and llama

These South American animals are related to the camels of Africa and India. Alpaca and llamas were bred in high altitudes to carry packs, to use as meat, and to produce wool. The vast majority of the world's alpacas are raised in Peru by small, mostly native farmers in the mountain highlands. Alpaca farming became popular in America in the last decade as a cottage industry.

There are two major differences between alpaca and llamas: alpaca are herd animals while llamas can handle being by themselves, and their wool. Llamas do give wool, but alpacas were specifically bred for wool production.

Alpaca don't secrete lanolin, so their wool is hypoallergenic. It's soft as cashmere, shiny as silk, durable and warm as wool. For these reasons it's become a popular commercial fiber. Both alpaca and llama yarns are available commercially. It is often mixed with sheep wool, sometimes with a bit of nylon added in to make the yarn more flexible.

Silk

Silk production and its culture developed in China in the Neolithic period. Historically, while the poorer folk wore hemp linen, the upper classes wore silk.[98] China brought silk to Europe along coastal trade routes and the land route of the silk road.[99]

Most silk is made from cocoons spun by the Bombyx mori moth.[100] This moth lives on mulberry leaves cultivated in captivity. In processing, the cocoon's threads are unwound and processed into fiber.

---

98. Robinson, *The Great Book of Hemp*, 103.

99. Barber, *Prehistoric Textiles*, 17.

100. Schoeser, *Silk*, 60.

Silk has a lustrous shine. If you've ever worn silk, you know how luxurious it feels! It's light and breathable and wicks sweat away from the skin so it is fantastic to wear in warm climates. Silk can also be mixed with wool into yarn to make a lovely soft fabric.

Ethical considerations: in conventional silk the worm at the heart of the cocoon is killed during processing. Some producers market *Ahimsa* or "peace" silk. In this production method, the moths are permitted to exit the cocoon before it is harvested for silk.[101] However, when the moths later mate, their offspring are too numerous for the farms to feed, so the offspring die. Does silk produced with this method deserve to be called peace silk? It is a controversial topic.

Synthetics

The term "synthetic" is usually used to describe a material that has been manufactured. Synthetic materials comprise the vast majority of fibers available in big box stores. I started my fiber career with a deep disdain for them—so cheap! So bright! So artificial! But as I dug deeper into the sources of our thread, I started to lose my certainty. I've learned that synthetic yarn is widely available, inexpensive, flexible, and highly washable. It is recommended as a way to avoid the ethics of using animal and plant products. Today, I have a lot of synthetics in my yarn collection.

Rayon

Rayon was the first artificial fiber to be developed. Silk was expensive and difficult to produce, so the search was on for a manufactured alternative. The first patent for rayon was issued in 1892 as a patent

---

101. Cook, "Ahimsa (Peace) Silk."

for artificial silk.[102] Sometimes it's called "viscose rayon" because of the way it is manufactured. It's bright and acts like cotton as well as silk, so the manufacturers combined "sunray" with "cotton" to make the word "rayon."[103]

Creating rayon involves a complicated industrial process. The raw materials are wood pulp from trees such as pine and eycalyptus, from cotton residue fibers called linters, and from bamboo. These substances are bleached and treated with caustic soda to create purified cellulose. Quite a few things are made from purified cellulose; it shows up in food as well as in fabric.[104]

Rayon is blended with cotton and linen to make a fabric that is more flexible and more absorbent than the natural fibers. It's more absorbent than cotton and linen and wicks away moisture from the skin. Because it is made from cellulose, it is flammable like cotton and linen.[105]

Rayon yarns are sometimes called art silk. The great advantage of this yarn over natural yarns is its price. It's vastly less expensive than natural fiber, something that can make a big difference in larger projects.

For use in magical projects, a yarn's color is more significant than the material. Although plant-based, the qualities of the plants have been substantially altered by the manufacturing process. Since it has been handled by machines and people before reaching the magical workroom, it is prudent to cleanse magically before working with it. I have used it to good effect in projects requiring a lot of bright color.

---

102. Ewing, *Fashion in Underwear*, 101.

103. Kan, *A Novel Green Treatment for Textiles*, 22.

104. Reimer, "5 Food Companies That Serve You Wood."

105. Parkes, *The Knitter's Book of Yarn*, 333.

Nylon, polyester, and acrylic

Like rayon, nylon was also developed as a silk substitute, this time to replace the silk used in parachutes used in war. But unlike rayon, which is processed from wood and cotton, nylon is created entirely in the lab. Nylon derives from oil. We might call oil a mineral because we pull it from the ground like metals and stones. However, oil comes from ancient living creatures compressed under stone, so it is classified as "organic" or carbon-based.[106]

Nylon is used in virtually everything: clothing, rugs, umbrellas, parachutes, rope, dishes, toothbrushes. Turning oil into nylon is a multi-step industrial process. As a fabric fiber, it's strong, light, warm, and easy to wash. However, it is sensitive to heat, so you will want to be careful if you decide to iron a nylon handcraft. It shows up as a core thread in yarns using mohair.

Polyester is very similar to nylon but created with a slightly different process. It is used more widely than nylon in clothing. Both nylon and polyester are lightweight and easy to wash, and more flame resistant than cotton. Polyester is softer and warmer than nylon but less absorbent.[107]

Acrylic was also developed as a substitute for wool and has been used in sweaters and blankets since the early 1990s.[108] Like nylon and polyester, acrylic fabric is lightweight, easy to wash, and sensitive to heat. Unlike wool, it doesn't felt when it is washed (unless you really want to felt it and take extra steps), so you can throw it in the washing machine instead of hand washing it. Also, moths don't eat it![109]

---

106. Woodford, "Nylon."

107. Parkes, *The Knitter's Book of Yarn*, 44.

108. Utah State University Cooperative Extension. "Clothing Textiles, From Fiber to Fabric: Acrylic."

109. Brooks, "Washing Instructions for Acrylic Yarn."

Synthetic yarns are very widely available in a vast array of colors. They are often blended with natural fibers to increase flexibility and strength. You are certain to encounter them as you investigate thread and yarn to make cords.

Ethical considerations: rayon is produced from cellulose which means it largely comes from trees. It is a good way to use cellulose byproducts.[110] However, the ancient and endangered forests of Indonesia, Brazil, and China are being logged to provide grist for the rayon mills.[111] Rayon processing also generates water pollution and industrial waste.[112]

Nylon and acrylic are made in large factories that require a lot of energy. The fabrics themselves are made out of oil. The world is becoming painfully aware that oil is not a renewable resource. As we get closer to using it up, the methods used to extract it will become more difficult and costly. So while synthetic yarns are a cheap and plentiful resource now, they will likely become rare and valuable in future generations.

Choosing a Fiber

Now that we have some idea where the fiber comes from, we can make an informed choice about which materials to use.

- Is it better to use natural or synthetic thread?
- How feasible is it to make our own?
- What are some of the ethical concerns in fabric creation?

---

110. How Products Are Made, "Rayon."

111. McCullough, "Deforestation for fashion."

112. Schinzel, "Water pollution by waste products of cellulose and rayon plants."

Natural versus Synthetic

At first I thought, "Of course I want to use natural stuff," but the more I looked at it, the less simple it became. Nearly all the material used to create yarn comes from living or formerly living things, even synthetics.

All commercial fibers have some machine-made aspect. It is possible to find artisan yarn and thread that has only been touched by human hands; for that you need to search out craftspeople or make it yourself.

Buying versus Making

Is it magically better to buy thread and yarn or to make it? Some craftspeople raise sheep for wool, some spin the wool into yarn, and some dye it with natural dyes. Artisans sell organic and hand-dyed cotton and linen yarn. If you feel called to do so, you can learn any of these crafts. It's even possible to make your own silk too: buy silkworm eggs online, raise them, and process the cocoons into thread.[113]

I know several people who produce craft wool. I even know a woman who made a linen piece beginning to end. She grew the flax and then took it through the many steps needed to make it into a material that could be spun. After that, she dyed the thread with dye made from plants she grew from seed. Think about how magical that thread is!

Most of us are not going to make our thread or yarn—we're going to buy it. If you like the idea of thread made by hand and you don't have skill or time but *do* have money, you can buy hand-spun yarn from individual craftspeople. Your local or online yarn shop may have a relationship with local suppliers. Many farmers'

---

113. Mulberry Farms, "Care and Raising Tips."

markets seek out relationships with craftspeople working to build a local fiber movement. You can find this kind of yarn and thread online, just search the term "hand-spun wool" (or linen or silk) for sources.

Cost versus Ethics

There is an ecological and moral cost associated with every fiber produced today. What we are staring down is the industrial complex of fiber manufacture. Industrial fiber is inexpensive to the individual but costly to the natural world. There's a farm-to-table movement for food, but there hasn't been a larger scale farm-to-clothes rack movement yet. This is mostly because making clothing takes so much energy that industrial machines are likely to remain part of the equation. You can grow your own food—it's much harder to grow your own clothes.

Why does any of this matter? The way an animal is treated doesn't show up in the physical characteristics of the final material, i.e., its warmth, feeling, durability, and upkeep. One answer is that the animal's quality of life may reflect in the energetic signature of the wool, or at least in how you feel about it as you handle it.

Personally, I try to be ethical but am not a purist. I buy some local food. I also buy locally sourced fiber products. The wool that makes me happiest to use is a hand-spun skein with a tag bearing the name and picture of the sheep that grew the fleece. That sheep is eating grass in a field and living a happy sheep life. However, I also eat commercial food, I knit with commercial yarn, and I simply can't afford to buy only organic cloth.

If you want to be sure the fiber you use comes from sheep, goats, and rabbits treated ethically, there are companies that market cruelty free products. Search on "cruelty free" wool, cashmere, angora, and yarn. You can also choose yarn suppliers who personally visit the farms that supply them with fleece and yarn.

I make most of my projects from commercial yarn. A cord made from manufactured thread is still a magical talisman. There is no one true right and only way to do anything, including picking the yarn for your cord magic.

Tying Knots in Fiber

Cord magic incorporates knots. Some knots are meant to be permanent, while others are meant to be untied to release the magical energy stored in them. In general, if you know in advance you will want to untie the knot, remember to tie it loosely. Before you make the cord, test the yarn by tying and untying a knot in it. If it's too difficult to untie, switch to another yarn. As a knitter, I have "tinked" or unknitted many a row. The worst yarn for this is mohair! I stopped working with it altogether. Interestingly, synthetic yarns are easiest for me to tie and untie a knot.

Now that we have figured out how number and color shape the cord and what fiber we will use, we can dive into designing the intention of our cords.

seven

Purpose

A cord is always practical. You can tie things together with simple string. This utility makes cords the perfect vehicles for the magic of everyday life. Practical magic focuses on five specific areas:

- Protection
- Health
- Prosperity
- Love
- Spiritual aspiration

You may already know why you want to make a cord, or you may not have an idea yet. This section lists common magical outcomes. As you read through the section, one of the suggestions may jump out at you. Once the creative spark has been lit, you might find you have quite a few ideas for cords! This chapter includes a cord design for each of these five areas and a space for you to design a cord of your own.

It is always best to write your own intention in your own words. To get started, each outcome below has a sample sentence that you can personalize. You will speak this sentence before you start twisting the cord. If you can condense this sentence into one or two words, you can repeat them while you are doing the twist.

Some of the outcomes pair well with others. You can choose to add other purposes for the cord to round out the outcome.

Intentions can be general or specific; e.g., "I find a place to live" versus "I rent an apartment in a safe neighborhood in walking distance from where I work." If you have specific requirements, you can add them to your intention. The danger here is in getting too specific, limiting your options—to continue the above example, maybe the perfect apartment is on a great bus line that cuts your commute. A better way to phrase the purpose might be "I find a place to live in a safe neighborhood with a short commute to work."

Another thing to keep in mind when creating an intention is to keep the wording positive. The human mind has what is called a negativity bias, meaning that we hyper-focus on possible dangers. It's easy to identify things we don't want to happen, but it's hard to design a magical intention around preventing things from happening.[114]

Let's take the example of protecting a new car. We want it to remain as scratch-free as when we drove it off the lot. However, if we say, "This car will not be in an accident," we first have to imagine an accident, which triggers anxiety and unhappiness. Both the image and the feelings have started the process of manifesting the

114. Tierney, *The Power of Bad*, "Prologue."

accident. We now need to cancel out that image and its feelings, which is difficult to pull off. How do you visualize "not"?

That's why it's generally better to avoid using negative words and frame the intention in terms of a positive outcome. For example, we can make a protection cord for our new car and say "This car is protected," and visualize the car in pristine condition, feeling the happiness this image brings.

We can make cords for ourselves and for the children, pets, plants and livestock in our care. We have both the spiritual authority and the responsibility to ensure the welfare of ourselves and our dependents. As children grow and begin to make their own decisions, we can include them in the magical decision making too.

We can also make cords for our friends and loved ones. These are magical gifts that hold energy for the recipients to use as they wish, so the intentions bound up in the cord should be positive and stated in general terms. For more specific magic, it is wise and ethical to involve the person in making the intention, and where possible in making the cord itself.

How to Use the Cord

An important design step is deciding how you will use the cord. When you have finished making the cord, you can wear it, keep it next to you, put it on something, or give it away. If you decide to wear it, state the intention as you put it on. If you keep it next to you, state the intent whenever you see or touch it. If you put it on something, you can state the intent as you tie it on the object. In the case of giving the cord away, print the intention on a card and include the card with the gift.

Personal Cords

You can wear the cord around your wrist. You can use it to hold a pendant you wear around your neck. You can keep it in a pocket in a small bag for protection. If you carry a handbag or daypack, you can tie it to the handle or place it in a pocket.

Cords for Family and Friends

You can give it to them to wear or put in a pocket, or keep it as a focus for your magic for them. If you are close to them and they are comfortable enough to give you a strand of hair, you can wind this into the cord to strengthen the connection with them. For people in care facilities or wheelchairs, a cord can be tied to the wheelchair or bed.

Cords for Pets

You can attach the cord to a collar. For cats who won't tolerate wearing a collar, you can keep the cord in a safe place, for example tied around the neck of a statue of a cat goddess such as the Egyptian Bast, or on a house altar that holds protective objects for the home. You can also wind their hair into the cord to strengthen the connection with them. For pets in cages and aquariums, you can place the cord on or under their containers.

Cords to Protect House and Belongings

You can hang the cord on windows, doors, or the four quarters of the house. With a car, motorcycle, or bicycle, tie the cord around the rearview mirror or handlebars or tuck it into the glove box. For suitcases, purses, and briefcases, tie the cord around handles or place it inside a pocket.

Love Magic Cords

In addition to using a love cord to hold a pendant, wear around your wrist, or keep in a pocket, you can also tape it behind a photograph of your lover.

Commitment Cords

If you make a cord with your partner, you can keep it as a single cord. You can put the cord in a bag and tape it behind a photo of the two of you together. If you have a house altar, you can put it in a box on the altar. You can also cut it in half (by making two knots and cutting between them) and each keep a half.

Releasing a Commitment

If you made a cord for the commitment, you can use that; if you haven't, you can still make a cord for the relationship. To make the separation, you can cut the cord. You may decide to bury or burn the cord or throw it into a body of running water. If that's too much energy to process all at once, you might cut the cord and then put the pieces in a box until you are ready to continue the work.

As you can see from the list of possible intentions in this chapter, cord magic can be adapted for virtually any magical purpose. It moves energy into your life and clears energies that no longer serve you. It's important to state the intention clearly. If writing comes to you easily, you may be tempted to compose rhyming poems for your intentions. That's perfectly okay! However, it's just as effective to compose a single clear sentence. In either case, if you condense the intention to one or two words, you can repeat those while you're making the cord.

Protection

Safety is the most important priority. It's hard to focus on anything else if you don't feel safe. Cords make ideal protection talismans. They can be tied around people and objects to form protective circles. They're versatile and portable. People use cords for jewelry and to tie on luggage bags to identify them quickly, so the cords you use to hang your pendants or protect your luggage will blend right in.

To protect yourself, you can make cords to wear and also to magically protect the places you live and work. It's particularly important to protect yourself while traveling away from familiar places and people. You can also extend protection to others, including family members, lovers, and friends. Your children and pets literally depend on you to keep them safe. Finally, you can protect the stuff you own. This includes the contents of your home, your car and other transportation, and bags while traveling.

Personal Safety
From attack, injury, and misfortune.

- **Intention for self:** I am safe and protected from everything that would harm me.
- **Intention for others:** (Name) is safe and protected from all harm.

Protection for Physical Space
From burglary, vandalism, and elemental and natural events, including fire, flood, earthquake, and storm.

- **Intention:** This space is protected from all harm.

Come Home Safe

Travel and return safely for yourself and for others.

- **Intention for self:** I travel to (place) and return home safely.
- **Intention for others:** (Name) travels to (place) and returns home safely.

You can combine a "come home safe" intention with a "personal protection" intention for children who go to school or other locations. This is also useful for pets that go to kennels and that are let outside the house.

Stay with Me

To protect physical objects from theft.

- **Intention:** This (item) is protected from all harm, stays with me, and returns to me.

Exercise
DESIGN A PROTECTION CORD

Go through this section and pick one outcome. This will be the result you want from making your cord. Next, summarize that purpose in a single sentence. It can be a complete sentence, such as, "I am safe walking from the bus stop to my house," or it can be in shorthand, "Safe travel now!" If you have chosen a second purpose, create a statement of intent for it as well. Next, choose the fiber you will use, the number of strands, and what colors they will be. Finally, when you have created the cord, how do you plan to use it? Will you wear it, put it in a pocket, tie it to something, give it away?

Outcome	
Purpose phrase	
Second purpose phrase	
Number	
Color	
Fiber	
How I will use the cord	

Charm
PROTECTION CORD

This cord is my go-to design when I am working with people and in places where I don't feel physically or emotionally safe. I often add a carnelian bead to the cord for extra protection.

Outcome	Physical and emotional protection in a threatening place
Purpose phrase	I am surrounded by a shield of protection

Second purpose phrase	Allies come to my aid when I need them.
Number	Four
Color	Dark red, dark orange, purple, brown
Fiber	Cotton embroidery floss
How I will use the cord	Next to my skin concealed from view

Health

As physical beings, we are susceptible to physical frailties. Illness, accidents, and defect are a condition of life, not divine punishment, magical failure, or signs of character flaws. Health does not correlate with spiritual achievement or moral superiority. Every person has the right to find meaning in their own health experience, and no person has the wisdom to judge the meaning of a health experience for someone else.

The critique and dismantling of racism and sexism works to establish equity for all ethnicities and genders. The critique and dismantling of ableism and ageism is less well developed, yet each of us at some point will pull a muscle, run a fever, and grow a gray hair. The healthiest cultures in the world value all their members equally, from the very youngest to the oldest, the strongest to the most frail. Few of us are lucky enough to experience such a culture; most of us live in cultures that measure value by the ability to produce labor at the expense of human connection. Let us be clear: all human life is valuable and all of us deserve care.

When doing health magic for someone else, it is important to check in with them to ask what outcome they want. When my mother-in-law told me her doctor said she could live to be a hundred, I said "Good!" and she said "Why?" At the point when she could no longer walk, she chose to discontinue medical treatments and died peacefully at the age of ninety. I would have cheerfully pushed her in a wheelchair for the joy of her company, but that wasn't what she wanted for herself.

My coven has met every sabbat for more than thirty years. As part of our rituals, we do magical work for people who ask us for it. There is always—*always*—a wish from someone for health recovery, and that wish is almost always expressed clearly and specifically.

Health magic pairs well with prosperity magic. In some parts of the world, health care is easily available and inexpensive. In others—America in particular—health care is not guaranteed and is astonishingly costly; one illness can wipe out a life's savings, and healthcare expense is one of the causes of homelessness. As you design the cord, you may add a prosperity intention to the cord.

The sample intentions in this section can provide a starting point for thinking about what you want or speaking with the recipient of the magic about what they want. In health magic more than any other type, it is important to customize the intention phrase for every specific circumstance.

Maintain Health

- **Intention for self:** I am healthy and remain healthy.
- **Intention for others:** (Name) is healthy and remains healthy.

Long Healthy Life

- **Intention for self:** I am healthy and I live as long I choose.
- **Intention for others:** (Name) lives a long and healthy life.

Increase Energy

For general health improvement and specifically athletic training, e.g., training for a marathon.

- **Intention for self:** I am strong and my energy increases.
- **Intention for others:** (Name) is strong and (her/his/their) energy increases.

Recover from an Illness or Injury

For short-term illnesses such as the cold, flu, and pneumonia, and injuries such as broken bones, strained muscles, and physical operations.

- **Intention for self:** I recover my health quickly and completely.
- **Intention for others:** (Name's) health returns quickly and completely.

Manage Pain

- **Intention for self:** My pain decreases quickly and disappears completely.
- **Intention for others:** (Name's) pain decreases quickly and disappears completely.

Become Pregnant

- **Intention for self:** I become pregnant when I wish.
- **Intention for others:** (Name) conceives at the time of her choosing.

Easy Pregnancy and Successful Birth

- **Intention for self:** My pregnancy is normal and my baby is born safely.

- **Intention for others:** (Name's) pregnancy progresses normally, the baby is born quickly, and mother and baby are safe and sound.

You may add the names of the biological parents to the intention, e.g., "Jim and Tanisha's child is born healthy."

Menstrual Health

- **Intention for self:** My flow happens normally every month.

- **Intention for others:** (Name's) flow happens normally every month.

Some women experience pain, heavy flows, and irregular timing. This again is a case where the person receiving the magic should specify the outcome, and we should not assume the experience we want would be the one that they do. "Normal" doesn't mean "regular" or "painless"—it means normal for that person. If you or the person you are working for do wish for less pain, you may add in the "manage pain" intention.

This outcome can also cover a wish to avoid pregnancy. When crafting intentions, it is a best practice to avoid using negatives, as in "I do not get pregnant." Wishing for a normal monthly flow is a positive way to ensure you don't conceive. You could also say, "I remain child free."

Perimenopause Management

- **Intention for self:** My perimenopause passes as quickly and painlessly as possible.

- **Intention for others:** (Name's) perimenopause passes as quickly and painlessly as possible.

Perimenopause is a natural condition that involves physical changes. Some are quite uncomfortable, such as hot flashes and migraines. However, we may not want to avoid these altogether, because there seems to be a link between hot flashes and a decreased risk of breast cancer later in life.[115] This is a case where a general wish, such as "as painlessly as possible" works better than a specific such as "without pain."

The time frame of perimenopause varies widely, from one or two years to as many as ten. Many women wish this time frame to be as short as possible. Some women welcome the change; others wish to delay it and remain menstrual. In the latter case, you could add "perimenopause begins as late as possible."

Strong Mind and Memory

For students and lifelong learners.

- **Intention for self:** My mind strengthens and my memory improves.

- **Intention for others:** (Name's) mind strengthens and memory improves.

---

115. Goodman, "Hot Flashes Linked to Lower Breast Cancer Risk."

Restful Sleep
- **Intention for self:** I fall to sleep immediately and my sleep is deep, peaceful, and healing.
- **Intention for others:** (Name) has deep, peaceful, healing sleep.

The inability to fall asleep and stay asleep is so common that news feeds regularly carry advice on how to achieve it. Advice generally includes establishing a regular sleep time, avoiding caffeine before sleep, and putting down electronic devices. Putting on a sleep cord can be added to a going-to-sleep ritual.

Retain Capacity
- **Intention for self:** My body, mind, and memory remain strong.
- **Intention for others:** (Name's) body, mind, and memory remain strong.

Age brings physical changes that can include decreased mobility, memory loss, and difficulty in sleeping. These effects may begin earlier than we expect. It's never too early to add a retain capacity intention to all health magic.

Mental Health
- **Intention for self:** I receive the care I need.
- **Intention for others:** (Name's) receives the care she/he/they need.

Mental illness, including anxiety, depression, suicidal thoughts, and substance abuse, affects as many as one-fifth of the American population.[116] Only about half of people affected by mental illness receive care.[117] Mental illness still carries a significant social stigma and is a leading cause of homelessness. This is an important intention to add to your self-healing and other-healing toolkit.

Happiness

- Intention for self: I am happy.
- Intention for others: (Name) is happy.

Happiness here is defined by each person who is wishing it. Happiness for some may mean giddy joy, while for others it means peacefulness and a relief from anxiety. It may be a steady state, lasting for months or years, or it may come in moments during the struggles of life.

This is another area that carries societal judgment. How many articles have you read that tell you "happiness is a choice"? It's harder to be happy when you're homeless or ill. We may reach happiness through life circumstance or through work in therapy or meditation. It may be more useful to think of happiness as a kind of grace: it is a gift when it happens, and we are grateful for it; it is also one of the gifts we wish for the people we love.

Manage Chronic Illness

- **Intention for self:** I have maximum energy and minimum pain and remain in control of my life.
- **Intention for others:** (Name) has maximum energy and minimum pain and remains in control.

---

116. National Alliance on Mental Illness, "Mental Health By The Numbers."

117. National Institute of Mental Health, "Statistics."

Chronic illnesses limit energy and may cause ongoing pain. As many as one out of three women and one out of two men will experience cancer; where recovery is possible, it requires focused medical attention which is costly in time, money, and effort for the patient as well as their family and friends. Some neurological and immune diseases have no cure and involve progressive capacity loss.

The experience of chronic illness differs from person to person. Some may experience a quick decline and passage, while others may live with a condition for many years. The magical work here is to minimize pain, maximize energy, and allow the person to retain as much control over their lives as is possible.

Easy Passage

- **Intention for self:** I cross over when and how I choose.

- **Intention for others:** (Name) crosses over when and how they choose.

Death is a natural part of life. Fear of death is one of our species' great afflictions, and acceptance of death is one of its great liberations. I have supported many people through their passage, both young and old, and it is a sacred experience that has helped me to accept my own future passage. It is a great gift to offer this support to the people we love.

This intention can be added to the "manage chronic illness" intention in a single cord. It doesn't mean that the person will pass immediately! It affirms their power to make their own decisions when the time is right.

Exercise
DESIGN A HEALTH CORD

Go through this section and pick one outcome. This will be the result you want from making your cord. Next, summarize that purpose in a single sentence. It can be a complete sentence, such as "I am healthy and remain healthy," or it can be in shorthand, "Health!" If you have chosen a second purpose, create a statement of intent for it as well. Next, choose the fiber you will use, the number of strands, and their colors. Also think about how you plan to use the cord after creating it. Will you wear it, put it in a pocket, tie it to something, give it away?

Outcome	Purpose phrase	Second purpose phrase	Number
Color	Fiber	How I will use the cord	

Charm
HEALTH CORD

Although I stopped smoking thirty years ago, there is still some weakness in my lungs; spring colds often settle into my chest. I wear a health cord to speed up my recovery.

Outcome	Purpose phrase	Second purpose phrase	Number
Return to health	My cough clears up and my throat heals.	I recover quickly.	Five
Colors	Fiber	How I will use the cord	
Light yellow, green, blue, dark purple, white	Cotton embroidery floss	Wear it on my wrist until I am healed	

Prosperity

The one percent own jets and limousines and vacation houses. The rest of us balance what we want to do with what we can afford to do. Each of us defines prosperity differently but in general, a prosperous person can take care of their own needs and help others while understanding that everyone needs help at some point in life.

Sometimes when I read prosperity magic advice, I think, "Yeah, maybe that works for someone like you!" Gender, race, age, and our birth class deeply affect our access to wealth. We don't start on an even playing field.

I am privileged in some ways and not in others, as is true for many of us. I have been so poor that a quarter made a difference to me; I went hungry a lot. I have also been so prosperous that I didn't have to think about the money I spent, and I got there with a combination of privilege, work, luck, and magic. I also didn't stay there—prosperity changes with age and circumstance. I was not a better person when I was poor, nor was I better when I was well off. Any improvement in my character is due to self-reflection, education, community work, and meditation and spiritual work.

Financial status is not a commentary on our worthiness, work ethic, character, or magical ability. It's a fact of life that we need to manage just as we manage physical health, dealing with what comes, and doing our best with what we have.

The word "wealth" comes into Old English from the Germanic *weal*, or "well-being," a word that referred to health as well as physical riches.[118] True prosperity provides the means to support our health and happiness. We can work for a short-term outcome (finding money to pay a bill) or a long-term outcome (establishing an income or finding a place to live).

Attract Money

- **Intention for self:** The money I need comes to me.
- **Intention for others:** Money comes to (name).

Keep Money

- **Intention for self:** My money stays with me.
- **Intention for others:** Money stays with (name).

This is a protection spell. Of course, it is important to manage and save money at every stage of life and at every level of income. It is also a fact of life that circumstances can deeply affect our ability to hold on to the wealth we have built. One of my favorite prayers asks for protection from "murderous thieves," phrase that includes burglars and ruthless capitalists! "Money" here means any kind of

---

118. Ayto, *Word Origins*. "The now virtually defunct weal [OE] meant 'welfare' and also 'riches'; it was descended from prehistoric West German *welon*, a derivative of the same base as produced English well."

prosperity. You can substitute "wealth" or "property" if you prefer, or use them all: "My money, wealth, and property stay with me."

Cover Expense

- **Intention for self:** (Name expense) is paid.
- **Intention for others:** (Name)'s (specify expense) is paid.

A sudden expense such as healthcare bills, car or house repairs, or an unexpected trip can knock out a savings plan. This intention also works for expenses related to things we may want to accomplish, like a creative project or a vacation.

We may not know the extent of the expense all at once. For example, the bills for a hospital stay might come in over time. That's why it's important not to specify an amount, e.g., "I receive $1000," but to work for the full expense to be covered.

Acceptance to School

- **Intention for self:** I am accepted into the school of my choice. Or: I am accepted into the best school for me.
- **Intention for others:** (Name) is accepted into her/his/their chosen school. Or: (Name) is accepted into the best school for her/him/them.

This intention applies to every level of education from preschool to university. Parents may make the intention for younger children.

Successful Studies

- **Intention for self:** I succeed at my studies.

- **Intention for others:** (Name) succeeds at her/his/their studies.

"Study" here can mean formal education at every level, study for a trade or profession, in addition to continuing education for its own sake. Here are some additional ideas to add to the intention:

- I have the time to study.
- I have a place to study.
- I am able to concentrate.
- My family and friends support me.
- I have the right teacher.
- I learn quickly and remember what I learn.

Pass Exam (School and Professional)

- **Intention for self:** I pass the exam.
- **Intention for others:** (Name) passes the exam.

Formal education includes formal examination. Professionals also take tests to qualify for certifications and licenses; some tests, such as the CPA exam, are notoriously difficult to pass. Every vehicle driver passes both a written test and practical exam.

Some people are lucky enough to face testing calmly. Others face significant anxiety which makes the experience more painful and the test even more difficult to pass. In this latter case, it is helpful to add calming energy to the intention. "I am grounded, calm, and clear headed during the test."

The "successful studies" intention can be added to this to support preparing for the test.

Find a Good Job

- **Intention for self:** I land the right job for me.
- **Intention for others:** (Name) lands the right job.

To fill out this intent, make a list of the things you are looking for in a job. Do you want flexible hours, a steady schedule, health insurance, high pay, child care, a short commute, the ability to work from home? Rank these in priority order from first to last and add your top priorities to the intention.

- I land the right job for me and my hours are flexible.
- I land the right job for me and my schedule is steady.
- I land the right job for me with good health insurance.
- I land the right job for me with an excellent salary and benefits.
- I land the right job for me including child care.
- I land the right job for me with a short and easy commute.
- I land the right job for me that lets me work from home.

Keep a Job

- **Intention for self:** I keep my job as long as I want.
- **Intention for others:** (Name) keeps her/his/their job as long as they want.

This is another protection spell. Job security is difficult to come by. It is common for businesses to fail and corporations to lay off employees. A person in authority may target you for any or no reason, making advancement difficult, and even endangering your employment.

Workplace harassment is also common. You may add an intention that you are safe in your position. An unsafe situation can change when coworkers and superiors step up to help alleviate conditions. You may add this intention:

- My job situation is safe, and I receive the support that I need.

Succeed in Business
- **Intention for self:** I succeed in business.
- **Intention for others:** (Name) succeeds in business.

There are many ways to be in business. You can be self-employed, own a small business, or be an employee of a large corporation. The term "business" covers any means of earning a livelihood.

You can succeed by selling a lot of things or a few valuable things, making existing customers happy, getting more customers, or impressing your colleagues and employers. You may measure success by how much money you make, or how much time off you get, or how happy you are doing what you do.

You can specify any of these things in your intention. The simple affirmation "I succeed in business" is a good start.

Place to Live
- **Intention for self:** I find the right place for me to live.
- **Intention for others:** (Name) finds the right home.

The home may be a rented room, apartment, or house. You may be interested in buying a condo or a house. You may also live in a tiny house, motor home, or houseboat.

To fill out this intent, make a list of the things you are looking for in a place to live. Do you want a low rent or mortgage payment, a specific neighborhood, a particular school district, on a bus line, with a lot of space, including a garden or yard? Rank these in priority order from first to last and add your top priorities to the intention.

- I find the right place for me to live which is easy for me to afford.
- I find the right place for me to live in (neighborhood).
- I find the right place for me to live close to a good school (or name the school).
- I find the right place for me to live on my bus line.
- I find the right place for me to live with as much space as I need. (You can specify bedrooms, bathrooms, workspaces).
- I find the right place for me to live which has a yard (or garden).

Transportation

- **Intention for self:** I find the right (name vehicle).
- **Intention for others:** (Name) finds the right (name vehicle).

Transportation can mean a bicycle, motorcycle, car, motor home, or even a bus pass. To fill out this intent, make a list of the things you are looking for in a vehicle. Do you want a low price or monthly payment, high gas mileage, low total mileage, space for a number of people? Rank these in priority order from first to last and add your top priorities to the intention.

- I find the right (vehicle) very inexpensively.

- I find the right (vehicle) for a low monthly payment.

- I find the right (vehicle) with high gas mileage.

- I find the right (vehicle) with very few total miles.

- I find the right (vehicle) with space for (number of) people.

Travel

- **Intention for self:** I travel to (place) and return safely.

- **Intention for others:** (Name) travels to (place) and returns safely.

To fill out this intent, make a list of the things you want in this trip. Are you traveling with another person or a group? Do you want to spend as little money as possible? Do you want to be sure to see or do something in particular? Some people enjoy taking small or even large risks—is safety your top priority? Rank these in order of importance from most to least and add your top priorities to the intention.

- I travel to (place) with (person/group) and return safely. We get along well and enjoy traveling together.

- I travel to (place) inexpensively and within my budget.

- I travel to (place) and (see/do a particular thing).

- I travel to (place) and remain healthy and safe throughout the trip.

Gift of Prosperity

- **Intention for others:** (Name) is wealthy in all the ways they wish.

A prosperity cord is a lovely gift on its own or added to another gift, for graduates, newlyweds, birthdays, anniversaries, or just because you want to give a gift.

Exercise

DESIGN A PROSPERITY CORD

Go through this section and pick one outcome to be the result you want from making your cord. Next, summarize that purpose in a single sentence. It can be a complete sentence such as, "The money I need comes to me," or in shorthand, "Money now!" If you have chosen a second purpose, create a statement of intent for it as well. Next, choose the fiber you will use, the number of strands, and what colors they will be. Finally, when you have created the cord, how do you plan to use it? Will you wear it, put it in a pocket, tie it to something, give it away?

Outcome	Purpose phrase	Second purpose phrase	Number
Color	Fiber	How I will use the cord	

Charm

PROSPERITY CORD

Budgeting is my weakness. I'm constantly borrowing money from my savings account to cover an expense I forgot to add. This cord shows up in my magical rotation more frequently than I would like!

Outcome	Purpose phrase	Second pur-pose phrase	Number
The money I make this month covers my needs.	The money I need comes to me.	I manage my money to cover my needs.	Four
Colors	Fiber	How I will use the cord	
Dark green, light blue, dark blue, dark purple	Cotton embroidery floss	Tucked into my wallet	

Love

We use the word "love" to describe the emotion we feel toward a sexual partner, a marriage partner, a parent, a child, friends, pets, and the natural world. Our love for each has specific qualities and a unique experience. In each case, we use the word "love" to identify a sense of connection that is necessary for our well-being; in fact, the feeling is so necessary that we are willing to sacrifice some or all of our *own* well-being for the needs of the people and world we love. The first part of this chapter focuses specifically on a relationship with a partner or partners. Later, we include intentions for friends and family.

Romantic love conjures up images of Valentine's Day, a budding passion, finding a life partner. We expect a lot from romance! Our one and only true love should be our best friend, constant companion, faithful only to us. Not only that, but the relationship itself should be easy—the partner should "get us" without a lot of effort.

It turns out that the description of romantic love in novels and TV movies is a great fantasy but not a good blueprint for success. Building a lasting life partnership requires communication, compromise, and ongoing work.

As we grow and change in our lives, a relationship that worked well may no longer serve one or both of us. What does it mean when our one and only true love no longer loves us? The first time I fell in love, I thought I had found my twin soul, the one who would complete me and be with me for my whole life. When that relationship ended, I had to figure out a new way to think about love. I learned that there are many different ways cultures have organized life partnerships. For example, some cultures don't expect marriages to develop from the lightning strike of romance but instead are arranged by parents who look for responsible and compatible partners for their children. It seems that love can develop into marriage, or married partners can develop love over time.

Love is also not synonymous with sex. Physical attraction may develop into emotional attachment, but it certainly doesn't have to! Biologically, humans act more like our chimpanzee cousins, which have multiple sexual partners, than animals such as swans and cranes, which mate for life. This directly challenges the one-partner-for-life ideal. Some people expect partners to be sexually faithful and feel betrayed when they are not, others manage multiple partners ethically.

Sex itself is natural and healthy. It can be an enjoyable physical exercise, a way to bond with friends or partners, a spiritual experience. It can lead to pregnancy, chosen or accidental. Unfortunately, it can also open us to physical and emotional abuse. As you reach out for sexual partners, it's important to be ethical in your own relationships, which includes telling your partners about each other and protecting their physical health. It's also important to protect yourself physically, recognize abuse and draw boundaries, and take the time to heal when you are hurt.

If romantic love can be separated from marriage and from sex, what is left? Everyone has a different answer to that question. One way to look at love is that it makes a connection which provides mutual emotional support. Part of our expectation of romantic love is that our partner is our primary confidant and ally. That doesn't mean that we have to have only one emotional support partner. Have you ever known a couple that only did things with each other? It's a valid life choice and works for some people, but it's not a realistic goal for every relationship, and there are risks in putting all your emotional and financial eggs in one life partner's basket. It's normal and healthy to want time to yourself and friends of your own.

Legally in America today, we can marry one person, divorce, and remarry, a practice sometimes called serial monogamy. However, some of us may need or want to have more than one romantic relationship simultaneously. This is part of the normal range of human behavior. Polyamory encourages honesty and clear communication that can lead to healthy and happy relationships. If you and your partner(s) are clear, it's perfectly okay to make a cord to attract another lover!

Love can end well, or it can end badly. You and your partner may be able to part peacefully and remain friends. On the other hand, you may be left with a lot of anger and grief. Sometimes you need to let go of an old love before you can settle into a new one. In any case, making a cord for the relationship and then unwinding or cutting it can bring closure to the connection.

Most love magic focuses on receiving magic, but love is also given. At times you may find yourself dry and barren because you have not received sustaining love. Then you might work magic to nurture yourself. You may choose to focus on giving as a life path, learning how to love even in difficult circumstances, protecting yourself appropriately while becoming a channel for the free flow of the river of love which sustains life.

Finding Romance

- **Intention for self:** I am open to love. I make good choices and find the right person for me.

- **Intention for others:** (Name) finds romance when the time is right.

Ancient grimoires and modern spell books sometimes gave instructions for directing magic to a specific person to fall in love with the operator. Today, this is largely understood to be an unethical use of magic. Instead, we focus our magic on ourselves, working to attract a good match who treats us well, in addition to preparing ourselves to be good partners.

Active Sex Life

- **Intentions for self:** I have an active sex life.

This could be a workbook in itself! Each of us has a unique understanding of what sex means, what we enjoy, and who we enjoy it with. For a happy sex life, your emotional interest needs to match your physical ability and available partners.

The key to success with this purpose is taking the time to get clear about what you like and what you want. Spend a few minutes reviewing your experiences. What do you want to repeat, and what do you want to leave in the past? This review includes both the physical acts and the shape of the relationships, how your partners behaved toward you while sharing sex and as friends.

- I accept pleasure.
- I know what gives me pleasure.
- I clearly communicate what I positively want.
- I clearly communicate my limits.
- I find the right sex partner(s).
- I keep myself and my partner(s) safe.

Keep Love Strong

- **Intention for self:** My love with (name) grows strong.
- **Intention for others:** The love between (names) grows strong.

We mark relationship anniversaries to celebrate the joy of sharing our lives and our success in passing milestones. Each romantic relationship has a different story arc depending on our past experiences and the unique intersection of our character with our partner's. In general, however, romantic relationships tend to begin with an intense infatuation, an exhilarating high that can last a few months or a few years. When that glow wears off, the real work of building a shared life begins, requiring clear communication. Just as communication is key to a healthy sexual relationship, it's also key to growing a partnership. Knowing what you feel requires emotional intelligence, being able to recognize and name emotions, and then communicating them. Emotional intelligence also means recognizing your partner's emotions and needs.

You're going to have a fight with your partner. Everyone fights—it's not an indication of failure. In fact, it's a sign that the relationship is maturing. We negotiate the shape of the relationship through resolving conflict. This isn't obvious, but communication leaders know that the only win-win conflict resolution is to actually have the conflict. You can avoid conflict by withdrawing (in which case your own needs don't get met), or forcing a win (in which case your partner's needs don't get met). Communicating your needs and listening to your partner's needs gives the relationship a chance to meet both your needs, and to allow you to give to each other.

- I know what I feel.
- I communicate what I feel and what I need with honesty and kindness.
- I listen to my partner with empathy.

While arguments are a sign of health, it's also important to nurture your shared happiness. The balance of conflict to happiness determines the relationship's quality and longevity. Sometimes that means releasing the mistrust built up from previous relationships. You may have learned to reject happiness to protect yourself from the pain of losing it, so you may need to learn how to relax and accept the joy of the moment.

- I am open to happiness.
- I communicate my happiness to my partner.
- I create moments that give us the chance to be happy.

Supporting Each Other
- **Intention for self:** I support my partner.

As a relationship matures, we begin to understand the ways we can support each other. Having a partner means having someone on your side. There are the everyday trials: someone insulted you, cut you off in traffic, shouted at you. There are the everyday successes: you got a compliment, achieved a goal, made someone else's day. Sharing these with each other builds our trust in each other.

- I comfort my partner and share my partner's happiness.

There are more serious life events too. Families have milestones and crises: parents grow ill, siblings marry and divorce, children need care. Pursuing a career or establishing a business may mean putting in long hours at the expense of household chores and relationship time. At any given time, your partner may need understanding and support, or you may need more support and understanding from your partner. You may also need more support than your partner is able to give, so the intention can include the possibility of having additional support from outside the relationship.

- I support my partner through this life change.
- I have the support I need in this life change.

Commitment
- I commit to (name) as my partner.
- We commit to each other as partners.

Support builds commitment. The promises you make and keep to support each other can be the foundation of a commitment vow. You can make a cord to represent your own commitment, or make a cord with your partner to represent your mutual commitment.

Connect with Friends

- **Intention for self:** I meet friends who are right for me.
- **Intention for others:** (Name) finds the right friends.

Love isn't just about marriage and romance, it's about friendship too. Every human being needs other human beings to care about them. Every day there are people who cry out on social media, "Isn't there anyone out there who cares? I am so alone."

We might define friendship as a connection with someone who is not a relative or romantic partner. That doesn't make friends less important than family or partner, in fact they are essential to our well-being. They make up our chosen family. They celebrate our successes and help us navigate our losses. It is important to acknowledge the depths of our feelings for friends. Friendships also have a story arc; they can form, change, and end, or they can last through a lifetime.

Family means the people who physically bring us into the world and raise us from childhood to adulthood. These are our earliest relationships and in many ways pattern our life experience. Although you didn't consciously choose your childhood family members, they are part of your life. You can think about them magically in the same way you think about the friends who make up your chosen family. If the relationship with your family members is a positive one, you can draw on the connection for support. If your family member affects your life negatively, you can draw appropriate boundaries.

The right friend helps you live a happier and longer life. The wrong friend can plant self-doubt and affect your health. How can you tell the difference? A good friend has a positive outlook on life and listens to you without judgment. They initiate contact and follow up with you to keep connecting. In general, you feel better after spending time with them.

The word "meet" in this intention opens the possibility of connecting with others. Social media connects us with people who share our interests and who may be physically distant. Those relationships can develop through meeting one to one by video chat. Clubs and conferences give us real-world chances to connect with people physically. Stating the intention, putting it into a cord, and wearing the cord opens up the magical possibilities for those connections to happen.

• **Intention for self:** I am a good friend.

Friendship is a two-way relationship. Being a good friend helps us to find and keep the right friends. Being a good friend doesn't mean letting the other person dictate the shape of the relationship! If you find yourself hiding your opinions or deferring to the other person's wishes, that's a flag to re-assess the relationship.

What kind of friend do you wish you had? That's the kind of friend to be. Every relationship is a feedback loop. Here's a game: the next time you're in a checkout line at the grocery store, ask the clerk how their day is going, and then listen to the response, then smile and say something cheerful. It usually doesn't take long to lift someone's spirits. Asking your friend how they are and then listening starts the feedback loop.

A good friend will return the question—how are you? The challenge is to resist the temptation to present yourself in the best possible light. Instead, answer honestly—even if you're feeling low or defeated, or if you feel as if mentioning your good fortune would seem boastful.

Circle of Support

- **Intention for self:** I have the support I need.
- **Intention for others:** (Name) has the support they need.

There are times in every life when the load is too big for us to carry alone. We get sick, break a leg, have surgery. We lose a job, lose a home, get robbed. We lose a friend or a lover. We lose a pet; companion animals are so close to us that their loss can be devastating. Someone close to us dies.

This is a stress test for relationship. If someone close to you needs you, are you there for them? When you are in need, do your people come through for you and offer emotional and physical support? Supporting each other through the bad times strengthens relationships in real and nourishing ways.

Support may come from people we already know and people we don't. I have been amazed at the kindness of acquaintances who reached out with genuine support when I needed it; they are well on the way to becoming true friends.

Loving Parent and Child Guardian

- **Intention for self:** I am a loving parent/child guardian.
- **Intention for others:** (Name) receives the love they need.

Love is a basic human need, just like food, water, and air. Each child requires loving care and guidance while growing up. The child raised hungry, in dangerous places, or enduring abuse starts life with a shaky foundation—it's possible to overcome, but no child deserves this. Family is the first place love roots.

You can direct your magic toward yourself to support your own growth as parent and guardian. You can also shape magic for children not in your direct care who need support. In that case, phrasing the intention carefully is important. It may seem to you that moving the child out of their home or making some other specific move would be helpful, but a specific intention like that risks interfering with a family dynamic and the child's own wishes. Saying the child receives the love they need is general enough to allow for the right solutions to manifest.

Clear Communication among Child Guardians

- **Intention for self:** I communicate clearly with (name) about (child's) care. We keep (child's) welfare and wishes at the center of our actions.

Some of the most difficult conversations to navigate are the ones we hold with ex-lovers and ex-spouses who share guardianship of a child. It's okay and important to work for your own protection and peace in addition to the needs of the child.

Loving the Inner Child

- **Intention for self:** I have the love I needed as a child.
- **Intention for others:** (Name) has the love they needed as a child.

Some of us were raised in families that did not care for us well. Even the happiest childhood had some moments of lack. Our child selves still exist as seeds of the people we become. You can make a cord to nurture yourself as a child, giving yourself the support you needed then, and giving your inner child the support you need now.

Relationship Ending
- **Intention for self:** I part from (name).

Every relationship has a beginning, a sharing, and an ending. The length of the relationship and the reason for ending is unique to each partnership.

The romantic ideal promises that when we find a partner we can make a commitment "until death do us part," a phrase intended to refer to our partner's physical death, but lifelong marriage is rare. Another way to look at it is that every relationship ending is a kind of death. We are no longer the person we were when we made the initial commitment, and our partner is not the same person either. Understanding this can help us navigate any guilt we might feel that we didn't keep the commitment vow. Perhaps we did keep the vow, but the death must be acknowledged and the partnership ended so we both can move on.

If you and your partner have a commitment cord, you can cut the cord, together or separately. If you didn't make a commitment cord, you can create a cord representing the relationship and then cut it. As you cut it, say, "I part from you." You can add any of the ideas below to complete the intention.

- **Intention for self:** Our parting is gentle and we remain friends. I draw appropriate boundaries.

This parting intention works for romantic partnerships, friendships, family members, and children. Some romantic partnerships end well, with both partners realizing the need to move on and working toward maintaining friendships; to keep the parting gentle, you may meditate on the ways in which you will continue to support your ex-partner as well as the ways in which you will no longer relate, such as no longer having sex.

People who are the right friends for others may not be the right friend for you, and that's okay. There are also people who perennially take more than they give—their stories are always about themselves, or they expect you to track them down and pursue the friendship, or they put you down in subtle or overt ways. It's okay to draw the line with them. With friendships and family members, you may meditate on the ways you will no longer relate and how you are drawing and enforcing your boundaries.

- **Intention for self:** I remain safe and protected as I part with (name).

Some partings are more difficult. Your ex-partner, family members and friends may be angry and even violent. This is especially true where the partner has been manipulative or abusive. It's okay not to remain friends with someone who has harmed you. I have experienced abuse and have helped friends who were abused leave their relationship. If you are in this situation, I encourage you to know that you deserve to be safe; reach out to your friends and your community to help you be safe.

- **Intention for self:** My heart heals.

However well or badly a relationship ends, there is a hole in our hearts where it used to live. You may mistrust your ability to love again or doubt your own worthiness. The end-of-relationship cord can help you move through this experience.

- I am loving.
- I deserve to be loved.
- I give my love where it is cherished.

Helping a Relationship End
- **Intention for others:** (Name) parts from (name).
- **Intention for others:** (Name)'s parting is gentle.
- **Intention for others:** (Name)'s heart heals.

When partnerships end, we turn to our friends for support and our friends turn to us. You may be friends with a couple who ask you to help them both end the relationship. You may also have a friend who needs support without involving their ex. You can create a cord for your friends as a magic gift or create it with them as a way to process the experience.

Tapping the Well of Love
- **Intention for self:** I draw from the well of love.
- **Intention for others:** (Name) draws from the well of love.

There are many ways love enters our lives, through family, friendships, romantic relationships. The intentions in this section cover only some of the possibilities of love. A more general intention can keep the magical possibilities more open.

There are times when we seem alone, when our lives are filled with pain or criticism, and no relationship is nurturing us. Other times, the people around us shower us with love but we find it difficult to return the affection. In these cases, you may need to focus on the source of love within yourself. Giving love establishes a connection that makes it possible for you to receive love in return.

Exercise
DESIGN A LOVE CORD

Go through this section and pick one outcome. This will be the result you want from making your cord. Next, summarize that purpose in a single sentence. It can be a complete sentence, such as "Love is in my life," or as shorthand, "Love!" If you have chosen a second purpose, create a statement of intent for it as well. Next, choose the fiber you will use, how many strands, and what colors they will be. Finally, when you have created the cord, how do you plan to use it? Will you wear it, put it in a pocket, tie it to something, give it away?

Outcome	Purpose phrase	Second purpose phrase	Number
Color	Fiber	How I will use the cord	

Charm
LOVE CORD

I like to be helpful and to give support to others. At times I draw down my own energy and need to be supported, but it's hard for me to ask for support, nor do I always recognize it when it is offered. This cord reminds me that I do have people who care about me.

Outcome	Purpose phrase	Second purpose phrase	Number
I recognize and accept support.	My friends and loved ones support me.	My heart is open to love.	Three

Colors	Fiber	How I will use the cord	
Light red, light orange, light yellow	Wool yarn	Wool yarn	

Spiritual Aspiration

• **Intention for self:** My life has meaning and purpose.

• **Intention for others:** (Name's) life has meaning and purpose.

With protection, health, well-being, and love as our solid foundation, we can turn our attention to a meaningful life. Each of us is tasked with finding our own meaning. While some traditions interpret our magical purpose to be to develop ourselves as the best person we can be, others call for a connection with others to help them also achieve their purpose. For example, the Buddhist Bodhisattva vow renounces the final achievement of spiritual awakening until all sentient beings also achieve this goal.

Access Spiritual Knowledge

• **Intention for self:** The knowledge I need comes to me.

- **Intention for others:** (Name) has the knowledge they
   need.

Knowledge comes to us in the form of books, videos, friends, and flashes of insight. This is a good intention to make when starting on the magical path or when feeling stuck and looking for a new direction.

Meet the Right Teacher

- **Intention for self:** I find the right teacher for me.
- **Intention for others:** (Name) finds the right teacher.

You may prefer to learn from a teacher or from several teachers. Where a spiritual path requires initiation, you will need to have a connection to a teacher.

Find Spiritual Friends

- **Intention for self:** I am surrounded by friends who support my spiritual path.
- **Intention for others:** (Name) is surrounded by friends who support their spiritual path.

Taking on a new path may bring a whole new set of friends. It is also true that sometimes people changing spiritual paths find that their family and friends have a difficult time accepting this. We can work to attract support from our existing friends and from new ones.

Exercise

DESIGN A SPIRITUAL ASPIRATION CORD

Go through this section and pick one outcome to be the result you want from making your cord. Next, summarize that purpose in a single sentence. It can be a complete sentence, such as "I live a spiritual life," or it can be in shorthand, "Spirit!" If you have chosen a second purpose, create a statement of intent for it as well. Next, choose the fiber you will use, the number of strands, and the colors. Finally, when you have created the cord, how do you plan to use it? Will you wear it, put it in a pocket, tie it to something, give it away?

Outcome	Purpose phrase	Second purpose phrase	Number
Color	Fiber	How I will use the cord	

Charm

SPIRITUAL ASPIRATION CORD

I work as a teacher and a student in large groups of people and intimate circles *and* sitting alone in my meditative seat where I con-

template the ways spirit manifests in the world. This cord reminds
me that even when I am alone, I am surrounded by love.

Outcome	Purpose phrase	Second purpose phrase	Number
To experience the love of spirit every day	I experience, passion, excitement, inspiration, growth, peace and aspiration.	I recognize spirit without me and within me.	Nine
Colors	Fiber	How I will use the cord	
Red, orange, dark yellow, light green, blue, light purple, white, gray, black	Cotton embroidery floss	As a bookmark in the spiritual text I am studying	

Where our needs are met and our purpose is clear, life becomes
joyful. We can learn for the sake of knowledge, travel for the sake
of experience, connect with others for the sake of friendship. We
can explore the spiritual world and meditate on the great questions: how does the universe work, and what is my place in it?

eight

Knot Magic

K not magic is an important part of cord magic, so important that when I say "cord magic" people often assume I mean "knot magic." Personally, I think of cord magic as being the primary magic with knot magic as a way to shape it. But if you want to think of knot magic as the primary magic and the cord as the carrier, you could consider the twist of the cord as a kind of knot!

Binding and loosing is an old description of magic. Knots are tied for every conceivable purpose—to attract good fortune, bring lovers together, and keep misfortune at bay.

There are three ways a knot handles the energy of a cord. We tie knots to:

- make something happen;
- contain or hold an energy;
- store energy to be released later.

Knots Move Energy

A knot is a wish when we tie it to make something happen. Cords capture energy for long term results such as protection, prosperity, and love. A knot pushes more specific and immediate energy. As an example, you could make a cord for general prosperity and then tie a knot in the cord to attract money to pay a sudden bill.

Exercise
KNOT WISHES

Intention: Write a sentence describing your intention. Chapter 7, on magical purposes, lists many examples of intentions. Copy out the intention clearly on an index card. Put the date (including the year) on the card.

Pick a cord: Choose the cord you will use. You can use a cord that has already been made or create a cord specifically for that purpose. You can use a single-thread cord for a knot wish.

Speak the intention: Hold the cord in your hands. Speak the purpose clearly over the cord.

Tie the knot: Tie the knot loosely so that it can be untied easily. As you tie the knot say, "With this knot the wish is sealed."

Store the cord: Place the cord and the index card in a small cloth pouch or bag. You may carry it or keep it close to your bed.

When the purpose is accomplished: Success! The wish has come true. You've passed the test, now drive the new car, move into the new house, or have that scheduled lunch with a new friend. Then untie the knot and say, "The work is done."

You can then continue to use the cord for other purposes. You may also decide to unmake the cord.

Knots Contain Energy

We can tie a knot to make something happen. We can also tie a knot to prevent something from happening. The knot puts the energy on a magical hold, keeping the energy itself locked up within the knot. This magic is used much less frequently than knot wishes because it's tricky to get the intention right. In chapter 7, we learned that it is important to avoid using negative terms and to instead create intentions as positive outcomes. If you're thinking about preventing something negative from happening, see if you can find a way to express this as something positive happening instead.

That said, there are cases where the positive energy of restraint is useful. Instead of thinking of this as preventing an outcome, it's helpful to think about the knot as capturing something and containing it. It's not turning the energy aside but is instead putting the energy on hold.

Here are some examples:

- **Feeling on hold:** You feel sexual attraction for a friend but don't want to act on it. The intention could be, "My physical attraction is on hold and we remain friends."

- **Keeping a secret:** Something has happened that you wish to remain secret, or you have promised to keep a secret for someone else. The intention could be "This secret is tied in this knot."

- **Retaining capacity:** you wish to halt the progression of a physical condition such as dental disease, arthritis, a neurological disorder, or simple age. The intention could be, "My condition remains steady."

Exercise

KNOT RESTRAINT

Intention: Write a sentence describing your intention. Avoid negative terms like "not," "never," or "don't." Focus on the positive result you want—privacy, health, friendship.

Copy the intention clearly on an index card. Put the date (including the year) on the card.

Pick a cord: Choose the cord you will use. You can use a cord that has already been made or create a cord specifically for that purpose. You can use a single-thread cord for a knot restraint.

Speak the intention: Hold the cord in your hands. Speak the purpose clearly over the cord.

Tie the knot: As you tie the knot say, "This intention lasts as long as this knot holds."

Store the cord: Place the cord and the index card in a small cloth pouch or bag. If you are working to prevent something, you can use a plastic bag and store it safely with your other magical tools and talismans.

Review the intention: If the cord is keeping an energy on hold, you may review the intention occasionally to be sure it still serves you. Your friend may move away, or your feelings may change and you are no longer attracted to them. The secret is no longer important to you and you would feel better sharing it or you have been released from keeping it. Your health goals have shifted and require an intention to be stated differently.

If you decide to release the intention, since the cord has held it for so long, it is best not to try to repurpose it but to unmake the cord.

Knots Store Energy

Knots punctuate the energy of a cord. Just as we can tie a knot in a general-purpose cord for a specific wish, we can tie a knot in a cord to store its energy to be released later when we untie the knot.

Weather events are a great example. Sailors famously use knots to capture winds and release them. You can make a rain cord using the colors of sky and water. To use it, stand in the rain and tie several knots, saying each time, "This knot holds the rain." When your local weather hits a dry spell and you need to water the garden, untie one knot and say, "Gentle rain, come and fall." This is also an interesting way to capture the energy of events such as solar and lunar eclipses.

Another example is a love cord. Circumstances will separate you for a time from someone you love, a long-distance lover or a child. Make a love cord, then tie knots in the cord, saying with each knot, "I love you." The person who receives the cord can untie a knot whenever they especially wish to feel your love for them.

When capturing energy, you may have to improvise. Once when I was visiting Minneapolis, there was a terrific rainstorm. I had just been talking to some friends about how they captured rainstorm energy. Quickly, I dug through my suitcase to find any kind of cord and came up with a length of twine. I ran out into the rainstorm and tied three capture knots. I put the cord in a small plastic bag with a note that said, "thunderstorm, Minneapolis," and the date. When I got home, I tucked a length of red cord into my suitcase for the next time I have a chance to catch energy!

Exercise

STORED ENERGY

Choose a cord: For any purpose, you can tie a knot to hold the energy until you are ready to use it. You can create a new cord or use one you have already created.

Tie the knot: Tie the knot loosely so that it can be untied easily. As you tie the knot say, "This knot holds this energy."

Gift or store the cord: To gift the cord, you can place it in a small cloth pouch or bag. To store it, you may place it in a plastic bag with a note about the energy captured, along with the date (including the year) and the location if appropriate.

To use the cord: Untie the knot, saying "This energy manifests now." When all the knots are untied you can tie new ones. You may also recycle the cord if the purpose no longer serves you.

Tying a Knot

Knots range from simple, everyday knots to elaborate ritual constructions. When tying knots in cords, you can use any knot that you are comfortable with. This book uses three kinds of knots: the overhand knot, the double overhand knot, and the figure eight knot. This allows us to tie three different knots in a cord so we can tell the difference between them. It's helpful to use household twine or another sturdy string while learning to tie the knots.

Overhand Knot

It is very likely that you already know this knot; it is the one used most often in everyday life. To make an overhand knot, make a loop in the cord. Cross the longer end on top of the short end.

Insert the short end through the loop in the direction away from you. Pull on both ends.

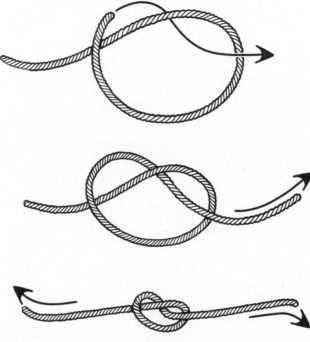

Overhand Knot

Double Overhand Knot

To make a double overhand knot, make a loop in the cord. Insert the short end through the loop, then insert the short end through the loop again. Now pull on both ends. You will end up with two knots very close to each other.

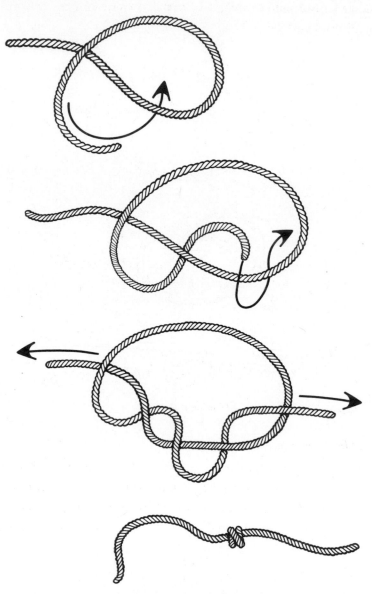

Double Overhand knot

Figure Eight Knot

The figure eight knot starts like an overhand knot. Make a loop in the cord. Insert the short end through the loop. But this time, loop the short end another turn so that the end is coming toward you when you pull it. Now pull on both ends. You end up with a knot that looks like a figure eight.

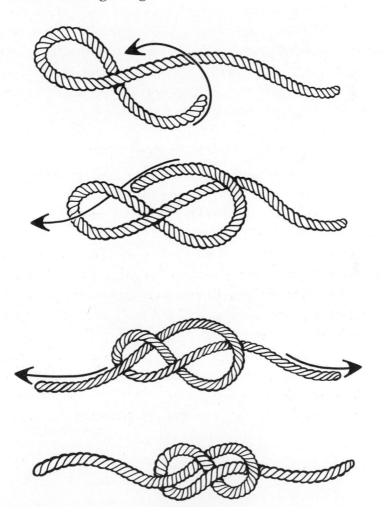

Figure Eight Knot

Tie the three different knots on the same piece of string so you can tell the difference between them. The double overhand knot is clearly larger than the overhand knot. You might tie the figure eight knot loosely so you can easily see the difference between that knot and the double overhand knot.

You can use the overhand knot for any knot charm in this book that calls for one knot or multiple knots for the same purpose. You can use these three knots for any knot charm that calls for different knots. The world of knots is fascinating, and you can add to your collection with how-to books and videos. One helpful book is *Why Knot? How to Tie More than Sixty Ingenious, Useful, Beautiful, Lifesaving, and Secure Knots!* by Philippe Petit.

Using Numbers in Knot Magic

We've used number meanings in this book to choose the number of strands in a cord. You can also simply use a single strand of yarn and then use your number meanings to determine how many knots to tie.

Another way to use number is to combine the number of strands with the number of knots to create your cord. You can use the same number for both the strands and the knots. For example, you could create an elemental cord with four strands, then tie four knots for the four elements.

You can also use a different number of knots in a cord to bring in an additional meaning. For example, you could create a cord with four strands to represent the four elements, and then tie seven knots to represent the planets associated with the days of the week.

Quick Reference
NUMBER IN KNOT MAGIC

Strands	Knots
Single strand	Number of knots
Cord with multiple strands	Same number of knots
Cord with multiple strands	Different number of knots

Unmaking a Knot

If you know you will untie your knot in the future, it's helpful to keep it a little loose. Tighter knots are harder to pick apart. In general, when pulling a knot apart, find where the strand overlaps and gently loosen both ends of the thread. You may need to insert a thin, pointed object such as a toothpick or pen into the knot to start the process of loosening the knot.

Some fibers are easier to separate than others. Generally speaking, the larger the fiber, the easier it is to pull the knot apart. Each skein of embroidery thread is actually composed of six separate strings wound together; when picking them apart, there is a danger of splitting the string.

Some cords develop knots accidentally when getting tangled with other jewelry and talismans. If possible, it's always best to untie the knot. But if the tangle is truly hopeless, it may be necessary to cut the knot with scissors. You may also decide to cut the knot as a magical act. Cutting a knot releases the energy stored in it. An accidental knot or one tied with a gentle intention will release its stored energy easily to be dispersed calmly into the environment. A knot that was tied with more serious intention may be holding onto a magical jolt. In the latter case, it's a good idea to cut the knot outside on the grass or under a tree, so the energy can be absorbed into the environment rather than zapping you or lingering in your house.

Exercise

CUT A KNOT

Clean and release the cord: Cleanse the cord in water as you did with the "Release a Cord" project (chapter 3). Untwist the cord as much as you are able.

Cut the knot: Touch the knot with your scissors, saying, "You have served your purpose, be released into the world." Holding the cord away from your body as much as you can, cut the knot decisively.

> **Tip:** A sharp pair of scissors will cut a knot more easily. Some kitchen knife sharpening devices include a scissors slot for you to sharpen the scissors blades.

Other Yarn Crafts

The focus of this book is on the magic of the cord rather than the craft of the cord. There are so many books and tutorials that teach fiber crafts that there's no reason to duplicate them here. However, if you already work with fiber, learning how to design a cord can open a whole new world of creativity. You can easily adapt the design methods in this book to create magical talismans and gifts with the crafts you have already learned.

Knitting and Crocheting

Knitting and crocheting create square pieces such as shawls and blankets; round pieces like hats and socks; and clothing like sweaters and vests that are created in several pieces and then joined together. We can turn these projects into magical pieces with our design choices. All yarn projects involve making choices in fiber and color and use numbers in counting stitches and rows. Each of these elements can provide meaning to a magical intention.

Fiber artists often make pieces to give as gifts. If you're making a blanket for a baby or a hat for a friend, you can speak the intention of the gift at the beginning of the project and meditate on it as you make the gift. Because of the way these crafts loop yarn, we can think of knitting and crocheting as making a series of knots that seal the intention into the piece.

As an example, one Yule I knitted elemental hats for people who requested them. I used shades of green for earth; light blue for air; darker blue for water; and warm shades of red, yellow, and orange for fire. I even made a lavender and purple hat for a person who chose spirit as their element! As I knitted the hats, I thought about the element and how well it fit the person who had chosen it.

Braided Crafts: Macramé and Wheat Weaving

Macramé and wheat weaving take natural materials and braid them together. Macramé can also involve making a series of knots in the materials.

Braided crafts use materials that are naturally tan and brown such as jute, hemp, and wheat or grass stalks. Unlike cloth thread, these materials are stiff and hold their shape when braided. Many projects simply use the natural colors of the materials. Some macramé artists use rope and clothesline cord, which comes in white.

It is also possible to find jute and hemp dyed in a variety of colors specifically for macramé projects.

Due to the nature of the craft, almost all projects use a limited color palette, often just a single color, so there's not as much chance to build in magical intent with color. However, braided crafts offer the opportunity to choose magically significant numbers. For example, in knotted macramé, you can choose a meaningful number for the number of knots across and also the number of rows down the piece. An elemental piece could have four or eight knots across and multiples of four or eight rows to make the complete project. You could make four hangings in each of the colors of the elements, or make one with stripes of color.

Macramé creates flat and round pieces that hang on a wall or basket pieces that hang from the ceiling. This craft pairs well with magical intentions for the house and household to protect the house, attract prosperity, and create a safe and welcoming environment for family and friends.

Wheat weaving is a folk art that developed specifically to bring blessings to the house. My favorite piece hangs in my living room. It's a twelve-stalk wheat weaving with a beautiful pattern that captures a wish for the house to be filled with happiness. It's worked like a charm for many years.

Weaving and Pin Loom Weaving

Weaving creates cloth by stringing rows of thread in a warp then passing threads called the weft through the warp to create the interlaced fabric. Weaving is the master class of fiber arts. It requires a loom of some kind, a teacher to show you how to do it, and time to master the techniques. I cherish the shawls my friends have made for me for the skill involved in their creation, their beauty, and my friends' expressions of affection.

Those of you like me who don't feel called to master weaving can still experiment with weaving techniques on a tiny loom called a pin loom. I got started with Florencia Campos Correa's book *100 Pin Loom Squares* and Martha Stewart's DIY Weaver Kit, which allows for adjustable square sizes.

This is a great way to use up little ends of yarn. Pin looms allow you to make a square of one color or multiple colors. The first square I made used the elemental colors, of course!

Quick Reference
USING COLOR AND NUMBER IN OTHER YARN CRAFTS

Number in knitting and crocheting
- number of stiches in a row or chain
- number of rows or chains
- number of inches wide and long of finished piece
- number of colors
- number of additions such as beads

Color in knitting and crocheting
- Single color of yarn
- Single skein of multicolored yarn
- Two or more skeins of different colors used in piece

Number in weaving
- Number of warp threads
- Number of weft passes
- Number of inches wide and long of finished piece

Color in weaving
- Color in the warp and technique which shows the color
- Single color in the weft
- Multiple colors in the weft

Knitting, crocheting, braiding, and weaving are all ways to bind cords together. We can think of all of them as elaborations on the basic twist and the basic knot.

With a good understanding of color, number, fiber, purpose, and knot usage, we are well equipped to design our own cord magic projects.

Part 3
Cord Magic Projects

So far we've covered how to make and unmake a cord and how to design a cord to achieve a particular purpose. Cords are such a versatile and creative tool that they form their own way to practice magic. The chapters in this section build out a cord magic practice.

Putting together a kit ensures that you have the materials on hand when you decide to make a cord. The time of day and season of the year affects magical energy, so why not capture those in a cord? Places carry their own energy too, and cords are a good way to capture it.

There are some life events that are so common they deserve their own projects. Witches use cords to cast spells and circles. You can also use cords to work with the Tree of Life and other ceremonial rituals. Finally are some projects that only cords can accomplish—binding us in marriage and in friendship.

nine
Cord Magic Kit

Walking into a yarn shop is like stepping into a rainbow. Shelves stacked to the ceiling are sorted by color and type of fiber. The feast for the eyes turns into a feast for the hands as you touch the invitingly soft skeins. It's great fun to hover over the embroidery thread wall in a fabric store and compare different colors until you find just the right combination. And even online stores offer pages of tempting colors and textures.

It's only fair to warn you that buying yarn is addictive! Most fiber artists end up hoarding chests, drawers, rooms, and even trailers full of yarn. We're always on the hunt for a stash buster that will use up the yarn—maybe this is why you bought this book! Don't worry though, you don't have to buy every skein in the store to make a cord. You can pick just the thread you want for the cord you've decided to make.

There is a happy medium between filling a room with yarn in case you might need it and buying thread every time you start a new project: you can make a cord magic kit. With careful selection, you can have the materials on hand to make a talisman for a specific purpose or for gift-giving. You can make the kit quickly using the quick reference guides in this chapter or spend some time enjoying the process of choosing color and texture. You can even give the kit itself as a gift.

In general terms, the process is this: first, choose the kind of fabric. Next, build the color palette, and finally, collect beads and pendants to include in the cord.

Choosing Yarn and Thread

Throughout this book, we've used the words "yarn" and "thread" interchangeably because you might be using either or both. Now it's time to look at the differences between them. Yarn is used to create bigger projects that can be used as a belt or hanging. Embroidery thread is used for small and quick cord projects to tie on people or objects. Yarn is available in fabric and craft stores and even in some superstores that carry some crafting materials. Embroidery floss is a bit more of a specialty item found in yarn and craft stores. Both can be found online.

If you're only going to use a few colors and want your cord to be larger, yarn is a great choice. Embroidery floss is a better choice if you find yourself making a lot of cords and you want to stock a large selection of colors. As a rule of thumb, a skein of matte cotton embroidery floss will cost less than a dollar. Commercial synthetic yarn skeins start at three dollars, while natural yarn can be ten to thirty dollars per skein.

Yarn

Entire books have been written about choosing the right yarn. In chapter 6 on fiber, we dove into the creation of the fibers them-

selves. We learned that you can buy yarn from commercial manufacturers or from independent artisans. The material can be natural, synthetic, or a blend.

Another important consideration is the width of the yarn. There
is very thin yarn used to knit socks and very thick yarn used to make
baby blankets. A good weight of yarn for cord magic projects is worsted or DK weight. This is the most common weight of yarn and
is very widely available. (Just a note that "worsted" is also used to
describe a fabric spun with a particular technique.)

Embroidery Floss

Embroidery floss is generally made of cotton. The most common
thread is called "six-strand" floss because it has six threads of the
same colors. You can cut a length of the yarn, for example a cubit
or 18 inches, and carefully pull off one of the threads to use it by
itself if you want a very thin thread. Mostly people do this if they
want to use embroidery floss like sewing thread. In cord magic, we
use the skein of floss as it comes with all six threads together.

Embroidery floss can also be found in a style called perle or
pearl cotton. In these skeins, the individual threads are twisted
together such that they can't be pulled apart. The twist gives the
thread a distinctive appearance. You may decide you like this type
of thread, or you can stick with the flatter appearance of six-strand
thread.

Cotton floss also comes in a variety of finishes. Regular six-
strand floss is matte, but you can also get satin finish which is shin-
ier (and more slippery). Metallic thread is created from synthetic
material that shines like metal. It is possible to obtain real metal
thread actually made from copper, silver, and gold. A thin wire of
the metal is wound around a central wire to create the thread. As

you might expect, real metal thread is significantly more expensive than synthetic counterparts. These materials behave differently than cotton thread and require some experimental fiddling to incorporate them into cords.

Embroidery floss skeins are generally 8 meters, which works out to 8.7 yards or slightly over 300 inches. This will make about 16 sections of one cubit or 18 inches. If you're making small cords, you can get about 16 cords from one skein.

Building a Color Palette

You can build your own color palette in embroidery floss or yarn for the elements, planets, and other magical energies that make up your cords.

Yarn and embroidery floss come in hundreds of different colors. To build our cord magic kit, we can start by focusing on the most common colors we will use. From there, we can branch out and add other color sets. The color sets should include some neutral colors, including white, black, beige, and brown. Adding these colors into the cord gives a background to support the other colors so we can see them.

Picking a color set sounds simple until you find yourself looking at a screen or row of bins with forty-two different shades of red! If you're picking them yourself, it's a good idea to get all the colors at once so that they match each other. Manufacturers and craft resellers package yarn and embroidery skeins together in color kits.

When you find a color you like, make a note of it! You can pick one manufacturer and use their colors, or you can mix and match manufacturers and artisan crafters. Each seller will have some way to identify the color which you can record in the worksheets in this chapter. For example, for my rainbow red, I might choose the DMC embroidery thread number 321 called "red," or DMC 304 "MD red."

Worksheet

RAINBOW COLOR PALETTE

A rainbow color palette is a great place to start. This color set includes red, orange, yellow, green, blue, purple, plus white and black. The shades of each should be bright primary colors.

Color	Manufacturer	Identifier	Color name
Red			
Orange			
Yellow			
Green			
Blue			
Purple			
White			
Black			

Worksheet

EXPANDED COLOR PALETTE

You can search embroidery thread online in the rainbow color categories or in the store sorted by shades. To expand the color palette, pick one lighter and one darker shade of each rainbow color. Embroidery thread manufacturers also include other shades to fill out the color spectrum, including browns, beiges, pinks, and grays.

You may also decide to add the tertiary colors coral, amber, chartreuse, magenta, turquoise, and periwinkle, which would expand the color palette to thirty colors.

Color	Manufacturer	Identifier	Color name
Light red			
Red			
Dark red			
Light orange			
Orange			
Dark orange			
Light yellow			
Yellow			
Dark yellow			
Light green			
Green			

Color	Manufacturer	Identifier	Color name
Dark green			
Light blue			
Blue			
Dark blue			
Light purple			
Purple			
Dark purple			
Red-orange (coral)			
Yellow-orange (amber)			
Yellow-green (chartreuse)			
Red-purple (magenta)			
Blue-green (turquoise)			

Color	Manufacturer	Identifier	Color name
Blue-purple (periwinkle)			
Beige			
Pink			
Brown			
White			
Gray			
Black			

You can make any cord in this book using this expanded palette, but you aren't limited to it. Add any colors you like to an individual cord or to your kit.

Worksheet
ELEMENTAL COLOR PALETTE

Decide whether you will use colors you have already chosen for the rainbow color palette or the expanded color palette for the elemental colors. If so, just fill in this chart with those choices. Or you may choose to use a different color thread for the elemental colors so you know that is the exact power you want to bring in.

You can also distinguish the elemental colors by choosing a different texture. Embroidery threads are available in metallic finish and glitter highlights.

What color is elemental water? Do you think of it as light blue, electric blue, navy? You can choose whatever shade you like to represent any element. It's easiest to pick all the elemental colors at the same time to ensure you like the way they all look together. Or you could try two or three different color combinations, make up a few cords, and see which you like best.

Element	Sample Color	My Color
Air	Yellow	
Fire	Red	
Water	Dark blue	
Earth	Dark green	
Spirit	Purple	

Worksheet
PLANETARY COLOR PALETTE

In some Western esoteric systems, each planet is associated with a color. These are listed as sample colors below. You can also choose your own colors based on the ones you've already chosen for the rainbow or expanded color palette. You might choose to distinguish the planetary colors from elemental colors by choosing a different texture, e.g., an embroidery thread with sparkle highlights or a metallic finish.

Planet	Sample Color	My Color
Moon	White, silver, or lavender	
Mercury	Orange	
Venus	Green	
Sun	Yellow	
Mars	Dark red	
Jupiter	Blue	
Saturn	Black	

Natural Dye Colors

In chapter 5 on colors, we talked about the natural substances that give dye colors. You can find wool yarn that has been colored with these natural dyes by artisan craftspeople. While sometimes on the pricier side, you can sometimes find small skeins of the yarn. Be careful when you search—it's common for commercial manufacturers to use natural-sounding color terms for synthetic dyes. Search in the craft marketplaces for "natural" or "plant-dyed yarn." And of course, you may also include yarn that you have dyed yourself.

Beads and Charms

In chapter 2 on making a cord, we talked about adding pendants and beads to a cord. This is such a broad subject that entire books have been written about it. Two good books to get you started are Navran's *Jewelry and Gems for Self-Discovery* and Loader's *Dreamstones*. (Rhea Loader was the person who first showed me how to twist a cord!)

To review, you can add beads and small charms to your cords in several ways:

- String them onto one of the threads before the cord is twisted.
- Sew them onto the cord with needle and thread.
- Slip them on the cord after it is twisted.

If you plan to add a bead after the cord is twisted, that bead will need to have a hole big enough to pass the completed cord through it. You might need to add small jump rings to the charms so you can slip the thread or cord through the ring. You can hang a larger pendant from a cord by passing the cord through its jump ring. Some craftspeople make cords to hang their pendants as an elegant upgrade from a regular satin cord or chain. To finish the piece, you can add crimp clasps to the ends of your cord.

You can use plastic or crystal beads in many colors. Gemstones and semi-precious stones are more expensive but are good for bringing a stone's energy to the cord. In general, the stone carries the energy of the planet whose color it shares.

You can buy beads of all colors, shapes, sizes, and materials in bead stores or online. You can buy individual beads, small lots, or entire strings of beads.

Here is a quick list of stone colors along with their planetary and elemental associations. Some stones can be found in several colors. For example, garnet is usually red, but it can also be found in green, yellow, orange, and even black! This list includes a stone's most common colors.

Red: Mars and fire
- Agate
- Carnelian
- Garnet

- Rose quartz
- Ruby

Orange and brown: Mercury and fire

- Amber
- Fire opal
- Sunstone
- Tiger eye

Yellow: Sun and air

- Citrine
- Yellow quartz
- Yellow topaz

Green: Venus and earth

- Aventurine
- Bloodstone
- Emerald
- Jade
- Malachite

Blue: Jupiter and water

- Aquamarine
- Blue topaz
- Fluorite
- Lapis lazuli
- Sapphire

Purple: Spirit
- Amethyst
- Sugilite
- Tourmaline

White and clear: Spirit
- Diamond
- Opal
- Pearl

Silver: Moon
- Hematite
- Moonstone

Black: Saturn
- Jet
- Obsidian

Storing the Materials

Once you have obtained the yarn or embroidery floss for your cord magic kit, you'll need a place to store it. This can be as simple as a shopping bag tucked away in a closet or as elaborate as a chest with drawers for sorting the colors. If you have expensive wool, you might consider storing it in plastic zip bags to keep moths from eating the fiber.

Embroidery thread will tangle quickly if you remove the paper sleeve that keeps the skein flat. For that reason, some craftspeople wind embroidery thread on cards. You can make these yourself out of cardboard or buy them from craft suppliers. Embroidery uses thread on a stitch-by-stitch basis, but a single cord uses up a lot of a skein at once so it isn't as important to wind it around a card.

Yarn can also tangle if the skein falls apart. Some people wind skeins of yarn into balls. If you buy yarn from a yarn shop, you may be able to ask the shop to wind it for you. Some people just take the yarn home and wind it into a ball themselves.

Embroidery floss manufacturers sell packages with all their colors, giving you more than four hundred colors to play with! How will you keep them all sorted? You might label boxes or drawers with the rainbow colors for an initial sort. Or you can sort the colors into their palettes, rainbow, extended, elemental, and planetary associations.

Beads and charms need their own containers. Craft supply stores and home stores sell small cases with compartments designed to hold jewelry materials.

Finally, you might tuck a pair of scissors into your cord magic kit. Fiber people find that scissors dull quickly with regular use, so it's nice to have a dedicated pair for cloth work. These scissors don't have to be expensive; really any pair will do—you'll just be using it to cut the lengths of cord.

Blessing the Materials

When you make a cord, you infuse the fiber with the energy of your intention. This is the most important action and what changes the cord from something decorative to something magical. It's perfectly fine to pull a skein from your kit and use it right away. If you want to step it up a notch, you can bless the materials you use in the cord.

There are two times you can bless the materials:

• when you place the materials in the storage container

• when you pull the materials out to use them

You can make blessing the materials part of your cord creation ritual. Another option is to bless the kit when you assemble it and bless any new skeins you place in the kit. Then the materials are always ready so you can make a cord at a moment's notice.

Exercise
BLESS THE MATERIALS

Prepare the surface. Choose a surface to work on—a small table, a corner of a desk, a kitchen counter. Cover this with a small cloth such as a handkerchief or clean kitchen towel. This should be in one of the neutral colors—natural beige, white, or black.

Set out the tools. Take a small decorative bowl and fill it with water. If you don't have a bowl for your magic, you can use a bowl from your kitchen such as a custard cup. Set out a small incense burner with a cone or stick of incense. You can use any incense you have on hand. If you're buying incense, pick one that means "consecration" to you.

Lay out the materials. Lay the skeins, beads, and other materials you have collected out on the cloth.

Activate the water. Hold your hand over the bowl of water and say, "Let this water purify and cleanse what it touches."

Activate the incense. Light the incense. Hold your hand over the incense and say, "Let this incense consecrate the materials."

Cleanse the materials. Dip your hand into the water, sprinkle water on the materials and say, "Let these materials be cleansed of all energies that have touched them so only the energy of the material remains."

Consecrate the materials. Wave the incense over the materials and say, "Let these materials be consecrated to the purpose of the intentions of the cords."

Give thanks for the materials. Hold your hands over the materials and say, "I thank the plants and animals and people who created this." Bring your hands to your heart and say, "I thank the earth for all the gifts that sustain my life and magic."

Put the materials away. You can store them in plastic bags, in a drawer of a plastic craft chest, wrapped in a small cloth in a box, or any other way you store your magical tools. Be sure to label them in some way so that you know that these are consecrated!

> **A note about the water:** Some people add salt to the water used in consecration; the idea is that salt represents the earth element, so placing salt in the bowl combines earth and water. Then when we light the incense and the smoke begins to rise we have combined fire with air, so we have brought all four elements to the ritual. The reason I don't use salt is that I pour the consecrated water out onto the earth when I'm done, and I noticed that water with salt in it can kill plants. Sometimes I add a pinch of dirt to the water for the earth element. Most of the time, I just use water and incense on their own.

Now that we've collected and consecrated our materials, it's time to start making cords.

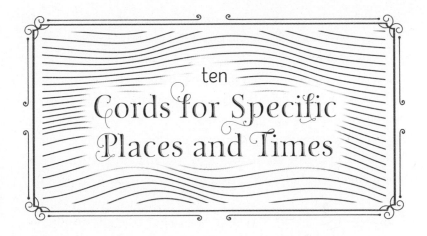

ten
Cords for Specific Places and Times

Magic connects with the flow of time and the energy of place. Making a cord at the right time in the right place enhances the cord's purpose. For example, for a cord to bless a new baby, you can twist the cord on a springtime morning under a blooming cherry tree.

What if the baby was born in autumn? You can always make a cord for any purpose anywhere at any time, so go ahead and make the baby a cord for a healthy and happy life. But if you already have a cord made under that cherry tree on an April morning, you can add the energy of that cord to the one you're making for the baby.

Cord magic is a flexible way to capture the energy of time and place. It's not the only technique that works; water does this too. I have a little water collection which includes a container I collected from an iceberg in Canada and a vial a Witch friend gave me from the last solar eclipse. You can use charged water to sprinkle a person, object, or place with the stored energy. However, building up an extensive water collection would take up quite a bit of space. Cords can be folded, labeled, and stacked in a box.

This chapter explores the energies of time to help you choose a day and season to make your cord. We will also explore ways to incorporate the energies of the elements and physical places in your cord magic work. You can make a cord in a specific place at a specific time to capture the energy of that place and time. You can then use that energy in any magic you do. You can wear the cords, put them in your home or work space or car, or use them in other rituals.

Chapter 11, "Cord Magic Projects," lists suggestions for creating cords for specific purposes. You can use the time and place cords you create to enhance the energy of any other cord project. If you have made a thin and long cord, you can simply add it to the cord you are making. However, adding a cord that is already made to a new cord can make it bulky and difficult to twist, so another option is to use the cord you have already made as a charging cord. In that case, you hold it in your hand along with the strands for the new cord while you speak the intention. The stored energy in the time and place cord helps to charge the new cord you are making. The projects in chapter 11 include suggestions for using a charging cord from this chapter.

Choosing the Colors

The cords in this book list color suggestions. You can also use the colors you see around you as you create the cord. You can bring your cord kit with you and choose the colors that match what you are experiencing. You can also fill out the charts in this section and use them to fill out the colors in your kit. If you find yourself making a lot of one type of cord, you can create a kit specifically for that purpose. For example, you might have a bag with all warm colors to capture the energies of noon, summer, and fire.

In addition to recording the colors you see, you can feel yourself into the earth and check out what energies you detect. Then you can pick a color that expresses that energy. For example, you might feel a bright hopefulness under a blooming cherry tree and add a light yellow or coral thread to your cord.

Creating the Cord

You can use the colors and invocations below or substitute your own colors and wording. If you want to use a different number of strands from the ones specified, you can take one of the colors out, double one or more of the colors, or add colors. For detailed instructions on how to twist a cord see "Exercise: Twist a Cord" in chapter 2.

Quick Reference
CORD MAKING TEMPLATE

Measure: Measure out the strands of thread or yarn.

Invoke: Hold the strands in your hand and speak the invocation.

Twist: Twist the cord and knot it.

Seal: Hold the completed cord in your hand and say the sealing phrase. Meditate for a moment on the energy of time or place you have captured in the cord.

If you're storing the cord for later use, you can label it by attaching a paper tag or putting it in a plastic bag and writing on it with permanent marker. Be sure to note the date, time, and energy captured (e.g., "spring dawn" or "thunderstorm" or "lunar eclipse").

Time

We can think of time as linear, running from the past to the future, or as cyclic, repeating like the sunrise happens each day. Magic links these two ideas. The journey from beginning to end is associated with the repeating cycles. This journey can describe the life cycle of a plant from seed to seed, or the life cycle of animals (including humans) from birth to death.

Quick Reference
DAY AND SEASON

Energy	Day	Season	Plant Life Cycle	Animal Life Cycle
Beginning	Sunrise	Spring	Sprouting	Birth
Creating	Noon	Summer	Flowering	Youth
Completing	Sunset	Fall	Fruiting	Maturity
Resting	Midnight	Winter	Seeding	Death

The above table maps the purpose of a cord to the time you make it. You can make the time of day cords in any season and make the season cords at any time of day. You can also substitute the time of day for the season. If you need to make a cord for a new beginning but the season is winter, you can make the cord at dawn. If you are able to combine day and season, for example making a cord in the autumn at sunset, that will strengthen the energy of bringing something to completion.

Each cord project below includes a table that lists suggested colors and leaves space for you to record your own color choices.

Charm
DAWN

Invocation:

Sun is up

New day starts

World is clothed

In beauty.

Sealing: Let it begin.

Dawn Colors	My Colors
Pink	
Gray	
Light blue	
White	

Charm
NOON

Invocation:

Bright of day

Height of sun

Strength of life

Shine!

Sealing: Let it grow strong.

Noon Colors	My Colors
Yellow	
Orange	
Red	
Beige	

Charm
SUNSET

Invocation:

Sun drops down

Day nears end

Time for home

And resting.

Sealing: Let it be completed.

Sunset Colors	My Colors
Dark red	
Dark orange	
Purple	
Gray	

Charm
MIDNIGHT

Invocation:

Stars shine now

And the moon

Lovely night

Is quiet.

Sealing: Let it rest.

Midnight Colors	My Colors
Dark blue	
Dark purple	
Gray	
Black	

Charm
TIMES OF DAY KNOT CORD

In addition to creating a different cord for each time of day, you can create one cord and tie knots at dawn, noon, sunset, and midnight. Search online to look up the exact time of sunrise and sunset, or tie a knot when you first see the sun and when the sun dips below the horizon where you live. Tie the first knot at sunrise and make it a larger knot such as a double overhand knot or figure eight knot. That way, you'll know which knot represents the time of day.

You can untie the appropriate knot whenever you need to add that time of day to other cords and charms. You can renew the energy by untying the knots and retying them on a different day.

If you see a particularly spectacular sunrise or sunset, you can capture it with this cord. This is a good cord to keep close at hand so you can catch the right moment during the day.

- **Number:**
- **Colors:**
- **Intention:**
- **Knots:**

Seasons

You can do time of day and season cords separately. You can also do a cord that combines the energies: dawn and spring, noon and summer, sunset and autumn, midnight and winter. If you are doing both time of day and season together in the same cord, you can speak both invocations but just say the sealing phrase once. You can also leave out overlapping colors if you'd like a smaller cord. For example, dawn is pink, gray, light blue, and white; spring calls for pink, light blue, light yellow, and light green. When you combine them, you can use just one strand each of pink and light blue and add one strand each of gray, white, light yellow, and light green.

Charm
SPRING

Invocation:

> A hint of sweet
>
> A splash of color
>
> Spring is a promise
>
> Tomorrow will flower.

Sealing: Let it begin.

Spring Colors	My Colors
Pink	
Light blue	
Light yellow	
Light green	

Charm
SUMMER

Invocation:

Long days and bright skies

A sense of ease and all is well

Move, make, grow, now!

Sealing: Let it grow strong.

Summer Colors	My Colors
Yellow	
Light orange	
Red	
White	

Charm
FALL

Invocation:

Cool days and colder nights

What is ripe is gathered.

Sealing: Let it be completed.

Fall Colors	My Colors
Dark yellow	
Dark orange	
Dark red	
Brown	

Charm
WINTER

Invocation:

Season of silence, moment of rest

Sleep, dream, heal, wait.

Sealing: Let it rest.

Winter Colors	My Colors
Dark green	
Light blue	
Winter Colors	My Colors
Dark blue	
White	

Charm
ALL SEASONS KNOT CORD

You can bring all the seasons together in a single cord, but note that it takes a year to capture all the seasons. If you'd like, look up the exact time of the equinoxes and solstices and tie the knot at that time, or you can tie the knot on any day that seems like the height of the season to you. Tie the springtime knot as a double overhand knot or figure eight knot, then tie the other knots between the springtime knot and one of the end knots so you can know which season each knot has captured. If you start with a season other than spring, just leave enough space so you can tie the other knots later.

You can wear this cord or place it on your altar or store it. When the second springtime rolls around, you can untie the first knot and retie it or tie another knot close to the first one to continue to capture the energy. You could also start a new cord and capture the seasons of each year separately.

- **Number:** Four strands
- **Colors:** Light yellow, light orange, brown, white
- **Intention:** "The power of the season is captured here."
- **Knots:** Tie a knot for each season. Say "(Name of season)'s power is captured here."

Phases of the Moon

The phases of the moon also bring energy to the magic we do. The waxing moon brings increasing energy, the full moon brings maximum power, and the dark moon brings the power of release and rest.

If you have any metallic threads in your kit, you can use silver, white, or red metallic colors in these cords.

Charm
NEW MOON

Invocation:

New moon

Waxing moon

Shine on me.

Sealing: Let it start.

New Moon Colors	My Colors
White	
Gray	

Charm
FULL MOON

Invocation:

Full moon

Power moon

Shine on me.

Sealing: Let it be so.

Full Moon Colors	My Colors
White	
Dark red	
Gray	

Charm
DARK MOON

Invocation:

Dark moon

Waning moon

Shining in darkness.

Sealing: Let it go.

Dark Moon Colors	My Colors
Dark red	
Gray	
Black	

Charm
MOON CYCLE KNOT CORD

You can tap into the power of the moon by creating a single cord and tying a knot at the new, full, and dark moons. You can do this as part of a group moon circle, sometimes called an esbat, or you can do it on your own. You may choose to tie the knot at the precise moment the moon enters the phase (there are many websites and apps that calculate this time for easy reference). These sites tend to list the new moon and full moon times; for dark moon work, tie the knot in the waning phase sometime between the full moon and the new moon, up to the last few minutes before the new moon.

To use the cord, you can hang it on the wall, place it on an altar, or keep it in a safe place. You can tap into the power of the cord whenever you need moon magic by laying it on your altar, wrapping it around a photo or object, wearing it around your wrist or neck, or untying one or more of the knots. You can reuse the cord and tie knots in it as often as you like.

- **Number:** Three strands
- **Colors:** White, red, black
- **Intention:** "Moon power is captured here."
- **Knots:** Tie a knot at the new moon, full moon, and dark moon. Say "(Moon phase) power is captured here."

Planetary Day of the Week

Each day of the week is associated with one of the seven planets known to the ancients. You can create a cord on the appropriate day to capture the energy of the planet.

Each planet is also associated with a number. You can create the cord using the planetary number of strands of the planetary color. For extra fancy work, you can use metallic colors for the planets, especially silver for the moon and gold for the sun.

Quick Reference
PLANETARY ASSOCIATIONS

Planet	Color	Number
Moon	White, silver or lavender	9
Mercury	Orange	8
Venus	Green	7

Planet	Color	Number
Sun	Yellow	6
Mars	Red	5
Jupiter	Blue	4
Saturn	Black	3

Note: silver and lavender are not included in the expanded color palette, but they are colors associated with the moon in the esoteric and folk traditions, so they are included here. They're also colors that are easy to find in embroidery thread or yarn.

Charm

PLANETARY POWER

This cord captures the energy of one planet at a time.

Invocation: Power of (the planet)

Sealing: (name the planet)

For each cord, hold the strands, say "hold the power," and then name the planet. For the sealing, hold the completed cord and repeat the name of the planet. For example: on a Tuesday take five red strands, hold them in your hand, say "hold the power of Mars," then twist the cord. When it is done, hold the finished cord in your hand and say "Mars."

Charm
PLANETARY KNOT CORD

You can capture the energy of all the planets associated with the days of the week by creating a single cord and tying knots in it on the appropriate day. Start this charm on Sunday and tie a large knot by doubling an overhand knot or by tying a figure eight knot. Tie the next knot on Monday and so on through Saturday. That way, you'll know which knot corresponds with which planet and day of the week.

You can place this cord on your altar, hang it on a wall, or wear it. You can also store it with your other magical cords until it is needed. When you need the power of a specific planet, you can untie its knot, then tie it again on the appropriate day to store the power until the next time you need it.

- **Number:** Seven strands
- **Colors:** White, orange, green, yellow, red, blue, and black
- **Intention:** "The power of the planets is captured here."
- **Knots:** Tie the knot on the appropriate day of the week and say "(Name of planet) power is captured here."

Place

Connecting with the Elements

What makes up the world? One way to think about it is to divide it into constituent parts or elements. This is an ancient human approach to comprehending the world and figuring out how to navigate it. It's both scientific and spiritual, exploring the observable world and mapping what we observe onto our experience of ourselves as more than the sum of our parts.

While it is not universal, many people in the Western magical traditions work with the energy of the classical Greek elements—air, fire, water, and earth. These elements describe the components of the physical world and map them to the spiritual world.

Earth describes soil and rock, the land we walk on. It also describes our physical bodies. Metaphysical earth grounds our spirituality as well. It is the essence of the solid, manifesting energy into visible and tangible reality.

Water evaporates from the surface of the earth, flies in the air as clouds, drops from the sky as rain, flows along the land to the sea. We drink water as an urgent necessity, much of our body is actually made up of water. Metaphysical water speaks to the flow of the body's energy and emotion which has physical, mental, and spiritual aspects.

Air is the atmosphere that covers the planet. We breathe air and walk in it. We can imagine ourselves walking on earth, but we can also imagine ourselves walking inside the planet, wrapped in the cushioning embrace that makes life possible. "Imagination" is a good way to describe air as a metaphysical quality. Air represents mind—our ability to solve problems and project the future that we rely on to build our cultures.

Fire is the most mysterious element. In some ways it isn't as much a substance as a process, transforming an object like a piece of wood into smoke and ash, releasing carbon and generating heat. In our bodies, fire describes the processes that transform air and water and food into energy stored as fat and used again to breathe and move. In the metaphysical sense "fire" is the energy that moves the universe.

We connect to the elements through the natural world. We also connect with them through using our magical tools. We can use incense for air, a candle for fire, a bowl of water for water, and a rock for earth. With these tools, we can create elemental cords to use on their own or to add to other cords. Here are simple consecrations for elemental cords.

Charm
AIR

Light incense and wave the cord through the incense.

Invocation:

Hold the power of air.

Air Colors	My Colors
Light yellow	
Yellow	
Light blue	
White	

Charm
FIRE

Light a red candle and wave the cord over it.

Invocation:

Hold the power of fire.

Fire Colors	My Colors
Yellow	
Orange	
Red	
White	

Charm
WATER

Dip the cord in a bowl of water.

Invocation:

Hold the power of water.

Water Colors	My Colors
Light green	
Light blue	
Blue	
Dark blue	

Charm
EARTH

Wrap the cord around a rock.

Invocation:

Hold the power of earth.

Earth Colors	My Colors
Light green	
Green	
Dark green	
Brown	

Charm
FOUR ELEMENTS CORD

You can capture the energy of all the elements by creating a single cord.

- **Number:** Four
- **Colors:** Yellow, red, dark blue, dark green
- **Intention:** "The power of the elements is captured here."
- **Knots:** Tie any number of knots. Untie a knot and say "The power of the elements is released here."

Powers of the Environment

Cord magic captures the energy of place. It starts with color, picking out the shades in the landscape around us. The next time you sit in your yard, walk to a park, or take a trip to a forest or beach, spend a moment sitting and observing the world. What color are the clouds at sunset? They can be pink, gray, orange, violet, with a bit of light blue. How many shades of green does an evergreen forest have? There's the dark green of the needles, the mid-range green of ferns, the bright green of the moss. A glacier-fed lake can have layers of shades from icy greens to deep navy.

There are other ways to connect with the energy of place. You can tie one end of the strands to a tree branch or a rock to hold the cord while you twist it. You can dip it in water and touch it to the ground. Sit and hold the cord while you meditate, extending your senses all around you to tune into the special qualities of this particular spot on the earth.

Charm
RIVER AND STREAM

Standing or sitting beside the river or stream, take a moment to think about what you ask the flow to bring you, and what you place in the water to be taken away.

Invocation:

Flowing water brings and takes.

Sealing: Hold the cord and say "Flow."

Flowing Water Colors	My Colors
Blue	
White	
Gray	

Charm
WATERFALL

Invocation:

Water under rock, through rock, over rock

Rising, falling, flowing.

Sealing: Hold the cord and say "Water falls."

Waterfall Colors	My Colors
Light green	
Blue	
White	

Charm
BEACH

Invocation:

Stones on the sand like clouds in the blue,

Wind whips the waves white,

Land, sky, sea, meet.

Sealing: Hold the cord and say "Waves move."

Beach Colors	My Colors
Blue	
White	
Beige	

Charm
FOREST

Invocation:

All the trees are one forest.

Roots entwined like fingers,

Like lovers, like family,

Standing together long enough

To know everything any of them knows.

Sealing: Hold the cord and say "Forest stands."

Forest Colors	My Colors
Light green	
Green	
Dark green	
Brown	
Black	

Charm
DESERT

Invocation:

Storm and silence

Sun by day and stars by night

Precious water and abundant life

Extremes teach us to live in the balance.

Sealing: Hold the cord and say "Desert teaches."

Desert Colors	My Colors
Beige	
Dark orange	
White	
Black	

Charm
MOUNTAIN

Invocation:

Straight cliff walls and gentle slopes,

Peaks reaching up to touch the bottom of the sky,

Mountain holds the power of the earth.

Sealing: Hold the cord and say "Mountain holds."

Mountain Colors	My Colors
Light blue	
Green	
Brown	
Black	

Charm
MEADOW

Invocation:

Blooming flowers and soft grasses,

Meadow invites us to rest and savor.

Sealing: Hold the cord and say "Meadow blooms."

Meadow Colors	My Colors
Light blue	
Light yellow	
Light green	

Weather Magic

One of the oldest and most common ways to use cords and knots is to control the weather. The principle is simple: twist a cord and tie a knot during a weather event you want to capture, then untie the knot when you want to encourage that weather to return.

Weather magic taps the power of wind, rain, and sun. On a hot summer day, you might wish for a cool breeze. A strong gust can fill a sail and push a boat along or renew still air. A hard wind can shake leaves from trees and refresh the environment. If you've seen too many days of rain in a row, you might long for a sunny day to dry things out. During a drought, a rain shower would be welcome.

Weather magic workers know that it's important not to overuse the power. You can make a local change for a limited time to clear the rain for an hour to hold a wedding or call a brief shower to water the garden. Keep in mind that all the weather of the world is interconnected—making larger or longer changes can have negative consequences both locally and in the whole system. Use the power you capture wisely!

Sun Magic

What is your perfect day? Most human bodies find a 70 degree temperature perfect—not too hot, not too cold. A bit of a breeze keeps the air fresh but not so much that it brings a chill. There's a bit of cloud to reduce the glare of the sun yet the sky stays bright.

When rains have drenched the ground and clouds have obscured the sky for days, a sunny day can bring reprieve—to let the ground absorb the moisture and plants and creatures enjoy the sunshine. When summer heat has scorched the world, a softer day can bring a different kind of relief. Here's a charm to capture the perfect sunny day.

Charm
SUNNY DAY

Sunny Day Colors	My Colors
Light yellow	
Light orange	
Light red	

- **Intention:** "Sunshine is captured." Tie any number of knots.
- **Knot:** Untie a knot and say "Sun shine."

Wind Magic

You can make a different cord for each kind of wind. This makes it easier to keep track of which wind you have captured. You can then tie multiple knots in the same cord to untie when you wish to release that wind.

Charm
BREEZE

Breeze Colors	My Colors
Light blue	
Light yellow	
White	

- **Intention:** "Cool breeze is captured here." Tie any number of knots.

- **Knot:** Untie a knot and say "Gentle breeze cool."

Charm
GUST

Gust Colors	My Colors
Light blue	
Red	
Orange	

- **Intention:** "Strong gust is captured here." Tie any number of knots.

- **Knot:** Untie a knot and say "Strong gust push!"

Charm
STORM

Storm Colors	My Colors
Blue	
Purple	
Black	

- **Intention:** "Storm is captured here." Tie any number of knots.

- **Knot:** Untie a knot and say "Hard wind blow!"

Charm
WIND KNOT CORD

You might decide to make a single cord and use it to capture all the winds. In that case you could use different knots for each of the winds, using a single overhand knot for a breeze, a double overhand knot for a gust, and a figure eight knot for a hard wind. Be sure you know which wind you are unleashing! It is a weather worker blunder to go for a gentle breeze and call up a storm.

- **Number:** Three strands
- **Colors:** Light blue, yellow, purple
- **Intention:** "The power of the winds are captured here."
- **Knots:** Tie a knot for each wind. Say "(Wind) power is captured here." When you want to release it, untie the knot and say "Wind blow!"

Knots:
- **Gust:** Tie the knot and say "Strong gust is captured here." Untie the knot and say "Strong gust push!"
- **Hard wind:** Tie the knot and say "Hard wind is captured here." Untie the knot and say "Hard wind blow!"

Rain Magic

Growing things depend on water. Too little water, too much water, or rain at the wrong time can ruin a garden or a crop. A little bit of rain at the right time can save a whole area. A strong rain cleans leaves and washes the air. Thunderstorms unleash a lot of power which can be damaging but also renewing.

Charm
SHOWER

Shower Colors	My Colors
Light blue	
Blue	
Gray	

- **Intention:** "Soft shower is captured here." Tie any number of knots.
- **Knot:** Untie a knot and say "Soft shower nourish."

Charm
RAIN

Rain Colors	My Colors
Blue	
Gray	
Light purple	

- **Intention:** "Hard rain is captured here." Tie any number of knots.
- **Knot:** Untie a knot and say "Hard rain fall."

Charm
THUNDERSTORM

Thunderstorms are powerful events that drench an area and bring a lot of water quickly. Lightning transfers negative ions from the atmosphere to the earth, fixing nitrogen in the soil and keeping the earth's electrical charge in balance. They can also bring destructive floods that uproot trees and cause mudslides and powerful winds that break branches and knock down power lines. Once unleashed, a thunderstorm runs its course. Be sure to manage this power carefully.

Shower Colors	My Colors
Dark blue	
Purple	
Black	

- **Intention:** "Thunderstorm is captured here." Tie any number of knots.
- **Knot:** Untie a knot and say "Thunderstorm burst!"

Now that we have a stock of cords related to times and places, we can use them in specific cord magic projects.

eleven
Cord Magic Projects

The projects in this section use strands of yarn or embroidery floss to create magical cords. If you have started with this chapter, the previous chapters in this book explore each of the design choices in depth.

Fiber: Can be natural or synthetic. Yarn is usually a blend of fibers; embroidery floss is usually made of cotton.

Number: Some projects use a specific number of strands for the meaning of the number. Otherwise, the projects use three or four strands.

Color: Each project contains suggestions for the color of the strands.

Each of these projects can be customized using the worksheets in this book. You can photocopy the worksheets and fill them out to create your own workbook. Then you can use your own number, color, and fabric meanings to choose the materials for each cord project.

Creating the Cord

Making a cord is so easy and quick—you can create a cord in the time it takes to read this section! Once you have made a cord or two, you will have the procedure down.

You can create the cord on a day, hour, season, or phase of the moon that will add to the cord's strength. Chapter 10 explores time in detail to help you select your desired timing. If you have created a cord to capture these energies, however, you can use this as a charging cord as described below.

Choose the intention

It's a good idea to write out the intention you will twist into the cord in your own words. Chapter 7 has dozens of examples you can customize for your intention. The projects below also have suggestions for intention phrases.

Lay out the materials

Choose the colors, measure and cut the strands. Add any beads you intend to wind into the cord as you make it.

Bless the materials

This is an optional step. You can bless the strands and the other items you will use to create the cord. There is a material blessing rite in chapter 9 called "Exercise: Bless the Materials." If you have already blessed the materials when you assembled your kit, you don't need to do it again.

Place and time energy

If you have created any of the cords listed in chapter 10, "Specific Times and Places," you can add the energy from that cord into the projects in this chapter. It is a charging cord because it charges the new cord with the energy already captured. If the charging cord is long and thin enough, you can simply add it to the cord you are creating.

Another option is to hold it in your hand along with the new strands. Repeat the sealing phrase you used to create the charging cord. For example, you can hold a springtime or dawn cord and say, "Let it begin." Next, set the charging cord aside to use again in another project.

Speak the intention

Read the intention out loud just before you start the twist. Take a moment to hold the strands and impart your intention into the cord.

Twist the cord

The section "Exercise: Twist a Cord" in chapter 2, "Making a Cord," has detailed instructions on how to do the twist. Remember to knot the ends when you have completed the twist to secure it.

Complete the cord

As an option, you can add beads or pendants to the cord.

Seal the cord

Hold the completed cord in your hand and repeat the intention. Spend a moment visualizing and feeling the result you want.

You can fill out the template below before making the cord to assemble all the materials you need. After you make the cord, you can add the data about when you created it so that you have a good record of the project

Worksheet
CORD MAGIC PROJECT

Yarn/thread used	
Number of strands	
Colors	
Intention	
Charging cord	
Day of week	
Date	
Time	
Phase of moon	

Tip: Record this information on a sheet of paper or an index card so that you can tape small samples of the strands to the card. That way, you'll be able to match those colors to your cords in case you need to identify them later.

Life Change Magic

When we are happy, we want our lives to continue just as they are. When calamity strikes, we want to resolve the difficulty and return to peace and prosperity. Then there are the normal moments of transition from one phase of life to another. The projects in this section focus on those moments of change to ward off difficulty, establish peace and prosperity, and support a successful change.

As always, you can change the colors and number of the strands and the wording of the intention. These intentions are written as if you are making them for yourself; to make cords to give as gifts, adapt the wording and substitute the name of the person you are gifting.

Charm
CREATIVE LIFE

- **Number:** Three strands for creation
- **Colors:** Dark yellow for inspiration, yellow-green (chartreuse) for imagination, dark purple for success.
- **Intention:** "I am inspired to create. I am surrounded by support for my creative life. What I create reaches the people who need and appreciate it."
- **Charging cords:** A cord from a place that inspires you.
- **Knots:** Tie one or more knots in the cord and say, "Inspiration comes." You can tie one knot for a big project, four knots for a set of projects, twelve knots for a project each month for a year, or any number that makes sense for your projects. Untie one of the knots when you are ready to start a project. Say, "I create!"

Charm
GRADUATION

- **Number:** Five. This is the four of completion, plus one more for the new path going forward.
- **Colors:** Dark purple for success, light yellow for optimism, yellow for happiness, light orange for communication, yellow-orange (amber) for confidence.
- **Intention:** "The right new path opens for me. I make new friends and keep the old."

- **Charging cords:** Water for the energy of flow, dark moon for endings and release, spring for new beginnings.

- **Knots:** Tie one or more knots for **endings**, saying "This is the completed energy." When you feel the need to release the old energy, untie a knot and say "I release the old." Tie one or more knots for **beginnings**, saying "This is the new energy." When you want to start on a new venture or make a new friend, untie the knot and say, "The new path begins."

Charm
FINDING NEW LOVE

- **Number:** Four. Partnership plus completion, two times two.

- **Colors:** Light blue for relief (releasing pain), pink for romantic love, light orange for communication, red for passion.

- **Intention:** "I release old pain to open my heart. When I make that space, new love comes to me. I am heard by my new love and I understand my new love. Our heartfelt communication fuels our passion."

- **Charging cords:** Noon and summer for passion, new moon for beginnings.

- **Knots:** Tie four knots in the cord, saying "This is the old pain, this is the space for new love, this is clear communication, this is passion." When you are ready, untie the first knot and say "I release the old pain." You may decide to write a journal entry or make a collage to work through the process of release. Next, untie the second knot and say "I make space for new love." You might capture your thoughts and feelings about the new love in a journal entry, drawing, or collage. When you have embarked on the new love, untie the third knot and say, "We communicate clearly." When you are ready to deepen your connection, untie the fourth knot and say "Our passion grows."

Charm
MARRIAGE

- **Number:** Three. Two lives make a new life together.
- **Colors:** Light red for love, dark blue for dependability, red-purple (magenta) for compassion.
- **Intention:** "My partner and I make a new life together. We communicate clearly and our love is sustained. We make a safe and nourishing home."
- **Charging cords:** Full moon for completion and success.
- **Knots:** Tie just one knot in this cord. After all, "tying the knot" is a term for marriage! This one you can pull as tightly as you like to keep the marriage strong.

Here are some ideas for using the knot in the cord. Right after the wedding, tie the knot in the cord expressing your wish for the first month of the marriage. Write it down! At the end of the month, untie the knot while thinking about how the month unfolded. Let your meditation guide you to your wish for the second month. Keep making a wish a month for the first year.

After the first year, make a wish for the next six months. Be sure to write it down and put it with the cord along with a calendar note to check the cord. Make a second wish for the next six months.

After that, you can make a wish a year. Be sure to pick a durable fiber for this cord so it will stay strong over time.

Charm
BUILDING A FAMILY

- **Number:** Three for the triad, two parents plus children. If there are more parents or children, add threads for each one.
- **Colors:** Green for health, dark orange for protection, dark red for the blood of life.
- **Intention:** "A child enters my life" or "children enter my life."
- **Charging cords:** Dawn, spring, and new moon for new beginnings.
- **Knots:** One knot for each child.

You may choose to become pregnant or help a friend who is making that choice. This intention is spelled out in the section on health, under "Become pregnant." You might also decide to adopt or foster a child or children. You may share child-raising responsibilities with someone who is the legal guardian of one or more children. You can help friends who are working to adopt or foster a child or several children.

Charm
ESTABLISHING A HOME LIFE

- **Number:** Eight. The two of partnership, the four of the square, the six of the cube, and eight for the wheel of the seasons.

- **Colors:** Dark orange for protection, red-orange (coral) for hope, brown for support, green for health, dark green for prosperity, yellow for happiness, blue for peace, dark purple for success.

- **Intention:** "My home is protected, my family supports each other, everyone who lives here is healthy and safe, we are prosperous and happy."

- **Charging cords:** Earth for stability.

- **Knots:** Tie one or more knots in the cord saying "safety and happiness." Untie the knot when you wish to renew the energy in the family and say "This family is safe and happy." One way to work the charm is to make twelve knots and release one of them each month.

Charm
TRANSITIONS

- **Number:** Nine for the number of magic.

- **Colors:** Dark red for life, blue-green (turquoise) for wisdom, dark orange for protection, blue-purple (periwinkle) for serenity, brown for support, orange for excitement, light green for new growth, light purple for aspiration, yellow for happiness.

- **Intention:** "I navigate this transition successfully into my new life."

- **Charging cords:** Winter and midnight for endings, spring and new moon for beginnings.

- **Knots:** Tie three knots in the cord. With the first knot say "Begin," with the second knot say "Continue," and with the third knot say "Complete." When you are ready, untie the first knot and say "The transition begins." With the second knot, say "The transition continues." With the third and final knot, say "The transition is complete."

———

This cord is for support in navigating any transition: starting or ending a relationship, a change in health, moving out or moving in, leaving a job or starting a new one, establishing or closing a business, joining or leaving a group, retiring, or supporting a senior.

Witchcraft Cord Magic

Witches use cords! When I was initiated as a first-degree Witch, the coven took my measure. I've taken the measure of every initiate I made too (I give them back to the initiate). I was taught to wear a large cord around my waist with the colors of my tradition—red, white, and blue. I know Witches who wear red, white, and black tradition cords. Witches use a cord to measure out the diameter of the magic circle and also to cast spells. The most famous spell is the nine-knot spell.

Charm
MEASURE

In *The Inner Mysteries,* Janet Farrar and Gavin Bone give a description of how the measure works: covens would take the measure of the new initiate as a form of protection magic. The idea is that the cord represents the person. If the initiate broke their vow of secrecy, the cord could be used to send punishment magic. Farrar and Bone transitioned away from this practice and instead gave the measure to the initiate as a mark of trust and finally stopped using it altogether.[119]Although I do take measurements of initiates, I agree that the practice of using a measure for punishment belongs in the past. What I do is take the measured cord as a way to connect with the tradition but return the cord to the initiate.

Here's how it works: Using a skein of red yarn, measure out a length of thread from the initiate's head to their toes. After the yarn is cut, the initiate holds their arms next to their body and the cord is wrapped around their chest and arms; a knot is tied where the two ends meet. The end result is a thread measuring the length and width of the person.

Charm
NINE-FOOT CIRCLE CORD

Witches often meet in gatherings called circles. Most Witches today agree that the circle should be whatever size will fit all the members; however, some traditions call for the circle to be nine feet across, the number of magic. To make the nine-foot circle cord, cut a nine-foot length from a skein of red yarn. To use it, lay it on the floor to mark out the circumference of the circle. You can place markers at either end to locate the edge of the circle.

In practice, a nine-foot cord is quite unwieldy to use. You can use a cord half that size and mark the radius of the circle instead. Measure a 4.5-foot length from a skein of red yarn. Anchor one end of the cord on the floor in the center of a room—put something heavy on it or tie it to a chair leg, or have someone hold it. Now walk in a circle around the space. Put markers on the quarters so you know where the circle lies.

---

119. Janet Farrar, *The Inner Mysteries*.

Charm
WITCH CORD

Initiated Witches often wear cords as belts on our robes. Generally a tradition specifies the color of the cords: the most common are white, red, and black, choices that resonate with the oldest colors of cord magic.

It takes a little bit of thought to make a cord that is bulky and long enough to act as a belt. This is a project where macramé works well. I have made a twisted belt cord for an initiate. For a three-foot belt, the strands need to be about nine feet long—it took five of us to stretch out the strands and wind them!

- **Number:** Three
- **Colors:** White, red, black
- **Intention:** "I call on the ancestors, the Goddess and the God, and the powers of the elementals to bless this cord."
- **Knots:** You can tie one or more knots in this cord for any purpose.

Charm
NINE-KNOT SPELL

Another use for the nine-foot cord is the nine-knot spell. Tie nine knots while concentrating on what you want to happen. You can tie them on the waxing moon to make things happen, like increasing prosperity and health, or tie them during the waning moon to send things out of your life, like illness and worry. In *The Complete Book of Witchcraft,* Raymond Buckland gives his version of the spell, along with the order in which to tie the knots.[120]

---

120. Buckland, "Cord Magick," *The Complete Book of Witchcraft,* 162.

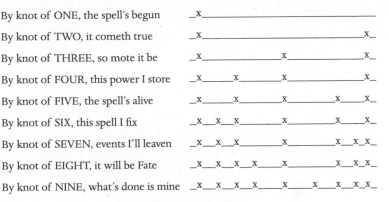

By knot of ONE, the spell's begun

By knot of TWO, it cometh true

By knot of THREE, so mote it be

By knot of FOUR, this power I store

By knot of FIVE, the spell's alive

By knot of SIX, this spell I fix

By knot of SEVEN, events I'll leaven

By knot of EIGHT, it will be Fate

By knot of NINE, what's done is mine

Nine-Knot Spell

Charm
WITCHES' LADDER

In 1878, an old house in Somerset, England, was dismantled. Workers found curiosities in the attic—an old chair, six brooms, and a length of string stuck with rooster feathers. The workers reported the chair was for Witches to sit in, the brooms were for Witches to ride on, and the string figure was a ladder to help them cross the roof. Thus the term "Witches' ladder" was attached to the object.[121]

The find was published in the *Folk-Lore Journal* and discussed by American folklorist Charles Leland, who was aware of a similar device using hen feathers. Gerald Gardner, the founder of Gardnerian Wicca, was also a member of the Folk-Lore Society. He and other Witches may have learned about it from that publication. The Witches' Ladder shows up today in books and on the web as a form of knot magic.

---

121. Wingfield, "Witches' Ladder: The Hidden History."

In addition to fiber, this charm requires feathers. While you may have collected feathers that crows, seagulls, and other birds have shed on your lawn, it's actually not legal to own a feather from any bird native to the North American continent. A century ago, feathers were fashionable; entire colonies of birds were slaughtered, so a law was passed to protect them. And since you can't prove that you didn't kill a bird for its feathers, it's not legal to own any.[122] However, you can use feathers shed by molting hens and roosters, which are traditionally used in the charm anyway!

First twist the cord, then insert the feathers into the cord. You can add any number of feathers. If you choose nine feathers, you can use the words of the nine-knot spell to direct the magic in the cord. I use the number 13, which has been associated with Witchcraft as the traditional number of Witches in a coven and the number of moons in a year.

- **Number:** Three strands

- **Colors:** Red, white, black

- **Intention:** "This is the cord for the Witches' Ladder."

- **Feathers:** As you insert the feathers you can say, "You are fixed as a rung in the ladder."

- **Using the ladder:** Speak the purpose you want to send out. Holding the ladder in one hand, walk the fingers of your free hand up the feathers. Say "I send this up the ladder," then count the feathers as you go, "One two three four five," until you reach the last number, then shout "DONE!" and flick your fingers upward.

---

122. Daley, "Five Things to Know About the Recently Changed Migratory Bird Act."

- **Storing the ladder:** Wrap carefully in a cloth and store with your magical items until you are ready to use it.

Sabbats

Making a cord is a lovely way to celebrate the season. You can make it yourself to capture the energy of the day. If you meet with a group, you can pair off and create cords, or you can all make a cord together and then divide the cord so you each have a part of it and a connection with each other.

You can put a specific intention into the cord for the season. You can hang it on the wall as a blessing. You can keep it until the next year and then replace it, or you can collect sabbat cords over time. Just be sure to label them so you know what they are. Whatever you do, keep a record of your intention so you can track your results.

Charm
SABBAT CORD

- **Number:** Four or eight strands
- **Colors:** See the chart below
- **Intention:** "This is the cord for (sabbat)."
- **Knots:** Tie a knot in the cord and say, "The power of (sabbat) is captured here." When you want that power in your life, untie the knot and say, "The power of (sabbat) is present now." If you haven't untied the knot by the same sabbat the following year, untie it and say, "The power of (sabbat) is released."

As an example, for a Brigid cord you can use two strands of white and two strands of red, and say, "This is the cord for Brigid

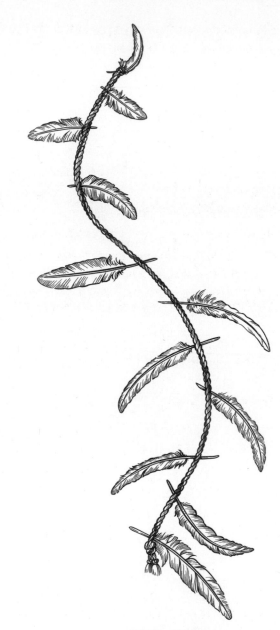

Witches' Ladder

this year." Tie a knot in the cord and say, "The power of Brigid is captured here." When you want that power in your life, untie the knot and say, "The power of Brigid is present now." If you haven't untied the knot by Brigid the following year, untie it and say, "The power of Brigid is released."

Quick Reference
SABBAT COLORS

Sabbat	Colors
Brigid / Candlemas	White, red
Ostara / Spring Equinox	Pink, green, spring colors
Beltane	Rainbow, all colors
Litha / Summer Solstice	Red, orange, yellow
Lammas	Orange, yellow, green
Mabon / Fall Equinox	Red, orange, brown
Samhain	Orange, black
Yule / Winter Solstice	Red, green

Charm
WHEEL OF THE YEAR KNOT CORD

One way to tap into the energy of the sabbats is to make a single cord and tie a knot in it at each sabbat. You can do this with a group as part of your regular sabbat ritual, or you can do it on your own on the exact day and time you choose. You can hang the cord on a wall or place it on an altar as it collects the energy of the year. Over time this can build up a powerful charge! The cord then adds energy to all the work that you do.

- **Number:** Eight strands
- **Colors:** White, pink, purple, red, yellow, green, blue, black
- **Intention:** "The Wheel of the Year is captured here."
- **Knots:** Each sabbat tie a knot in the cord, saying "(Sabbat name) is captured here."

Astrological Sign Cords

The sun enters a different sign of the zodiac each month. Your astrological sign is the sign the sun occupied when you were born. You can have a natal chart cast that maps the relationships of the planets in the sky on your birthday. This is a whole field of study in itself! If you know your sign or are interested in exploring it, you can make a cord for your sign.

You can make any astrological cord at any time. But if you can wait, it's great to make a cord during the month the sun is in that sign to capture the energy that's active in your environment at that moment. Because the astrological signs match up with the calendar, it's tempting to associate them with the seasons but these are different depending on where you are on the planet. For example, spring starts in February in my home town of Seattle, May in Minneapolis, and September in Sydney, Australia.

Every astrological sign is associated with three attributes: a planet, an element, and a quality. The qualities are cardinal, fixed, and mutable. Cardinal signs start the cycle, fixed signs stabilize energies, and mutable signs manage transitions. The worksheet below lists the colors I use for the qualities as an example, along with a space for your own colors if you prefer different ones.

Worksheet
COLORS OF ASTROLOGICAL QUALITIES

Quality	Sample Color	My Colors
Cardinal	Dark purple	
Fixed	Brown	
Mutable	Light orange	

Quick Reference
ASTROLOGICAL SIGN COLORS

Because there is so much color overlap, it's a good idea to have different shades of color for the elements and the planets. For example, you can see that Aries has two different shades of red—one for fire and one for Mars.

Sign	Planetary color	Elemental color	Quality color
Aries	Mars: dark red	Fire: red	Cardinal: dark purple
Taurus	Venus: green	Earth: dark green	Fixed: brown
Gemini	Mercury: orange	Air: yellow	Mutable: light orange
Cancer	Moon: white	Water: dark blue	Cardinal: dark purple

Sign	Planetary color	Elemental color	Quality color
Leo	Sun: yellow	Fire: red	Fixed: brown
Virgo	Mercury: orange	Earth: dark green	Mutable: light orange
Libra	Venus: green	Air: yellow	Cardinal: dark purple
Scorpio	Mars: red	Water: dark blue	Fixed: brown
Sagittarius	Jupiter: blue	Fire: red	Mutable: light orange
Capricorn	Saturn: black	Earth: dark green	Cardinal: dark purple
Aquarius	Saturn: black Uranus: purple	Air: yellow	Fixed: brown
Pisces	Jupiter: blue Pluto: white	Water: blue	Mutable: light orange

The ancients only knew the planets visible to the naked eye, so they assigned Saturn to Aquarius and Jupiter to Pisces. In modern astrology, Aquarius is also ruled by Uranus and Pisces is also ruled by Pluto. You can use either planet or both. The ancients were not aware of the new, outer planets, so they didn't assign colors to them. Suggestions are given here, though you can use other colors if you would like.

Charm
ASTROLOGICAL SIGN CORD

- **Number:** Three: one each for the planet, element, and quality
- **Colors:** The colors of the planet, element and quality of the sign.
- **Intention:** "This is the cord for (sign)."
- **Knots:** Tie a knot in the cord and say, "The power of (sign) is captured here." When you want that power in your life, untie the knot and say, "The power of (sign) is present now." If you haven't untied the knot by the same sabbat the following year, untie it and say, "The power of (sign) is released."

For example, for an Aries cord you can use one strand of red for fire, two strands of dark red for Mars, and say "This is the cord for Aries this year." Tie a knot in the cord and say, "The power of Aries is captured here." When you want that power in your life, untie the knot and say, "The power of Aries is present now."

You can add the astrological sign colors to any other cord to personalize it. An astrological sign cord also makes a great birthday gift.

Ceremonial Magick Cords

Ceremonial Magicians use planetary colors in their work. The adepts of the Golden Dawn expanded on the basic colors of the planets. They explored colors related to the planetary correspondences of the Hermetic Tree of Life based on the Hebrew Qabbalah. The visionary artists of the Golden Dawn, Florence Farr and

Moina Mathers, created the color scales in use today.[123] These were also the scales that Lady Freida Harris used in painting Aleister Crowley's Thoth Tarot.[124]

Here's how it works. The Tree of Life has ten spheres. Furthermore, the Tree exists in four worlds. Think of four Trees stacked on top of each other like a layer cake. The Golden Dawn system assigns colors to each of the spheres in each of the four worlds, for a total of forty colors. They named these four color scales after the court cards of the tarot: King, Queen, Prince, and Princess.

There are also 22 paths connecting the 10 spheres. In the Hermetic Tree, each of these paths is assigned to a planet, an astrological sign, or one of the elements air, fire, and water. Each of these paths also exists in the four worlds and is assigned a color in the King, Queen, Prince, or Princess scales.

It's hard to find an image of spheres and paths in the four worlds, but it's easy to make a cord with four colors! Making a Tree of Life sphere cord is one of the coolest things to do with this magic.

Richard Dudschus and David Sledzinski offer a free book called *Coloring the Classic Golden Dawn Tarot* (listed in the bibliography). They give the color correspondences for all the spheres and paths. You can use any other sources that make sense to you. Most importantly, you can tap into your own intuition to find the colors that work for you.

The Golden Dawn colors include combinations of colors and speckled colors. You may explore the world of fiber and find matches for each of them. The quick reference chart below translates these colors into the expanded color palette used in this book.

---

123. Dudschus, *Coloring the Classic Golden Dawn Tarot*.

124. Duquette, *Understanding Aleister Crowley's Thoth Tarot: New Edition*, 68.

To keep the correspondences recognizable for Ceremonial magicians, Qaballists, and esotericists, the chart gives the scales with the Golden Dawn names which reflect a male bias and are somewhat dated, you may feel free to rename them. As the spheres 2 through 10 correspond to the planets, the Queen scale for each sphere reflects the color of the associated planet. Spheres 1 and 2 are associated with the starry sky and with the ultimate reality, labeled here as "space."

Quick Reference
TREE OF LIFE COLORS

Sphere	Planetary name	King Scale	Queen Scale	Prince Scale	Princess Scale
1	Space	White	White	White	White
2	Stars	Light blue	Gray	Blue-green (turquoise)	Dark purple
3	Saturn	Dark red	Black	Brown	Gray
4	Jupiter	Dark blue	Blue	Light blue	Light yellow
5	Mars	Orange	Red	Dark orange	Light red
6	Sun	Pink	Yellow	Red-orange (coral)	Dark yellow
7	Venus	Yellow-orange (amber)	Green	Yellow-green (chartreuse)	Light green
8	Mercury	Light purple	Orange	Red-purple (magenta)	Light orange

Sphere	Planetary name	King Scale	Queen Scale	Prince Scale	Princess Scale
9	Moon	Beige	White	Blue-purple (periwinkle)	Gray
10	Earth	Light yellow	Dark green	Dark red	Black

Charm
SPHERE CORD

- **Number:** Four strands

- **Colors:** See the quick reference chart above

- **Intention:** "This is the cord for (sphere's planetary name)." Qabbalists may use the Qabbalistic name for the sphere (Kether, Chokmah, Binah, Chesed, Geburah, Tifareth, Netzach, Hod, Yesod, and Malkuth).

- **Knots:** Tie a knot in the cord and say, "The power of (sphere) is captured here." When you want that power in your life, untie the knot and say, "The power of (sphere) is present now."

Charm
TREE OF LIFE CORD

This cord takes the Queen scale or planetary colors and combines them to create a Tree of Life cord. Since white represents the first sphere, the color for the moon here comes from the Prince scale, blue-purple.

- **Number:** Ten strands
- **Colors:** White, gray, black, blue, red, yellow, green, orange, blue-purple (periwinkle), dark green.
- **Intention:** "This cord holds the power of the Tree of Life."

This cord is particularly good as a string for a pendant or to wear while studying the Tree of Life and practicing its rituals.

Special Projects

Here are two projects that don't fit into another category but stand on their own as magical works. The first is house magic, protecting where we live. The second is handfasting magic, binding our lives together.

Charm
HOUSE PROTECTION

Magic workers use talismans to protect our living spaces. Cords make wonderful protection talismans on their own. They can also be paired with other objects such as pentacles, stones with holes in them, rowan berries, and other objects with protective associations. The cords can be hung over doors and windows. They can also be placed in four places around the house to form a protective field.

North

- **Number:** Four for the square of protection
- **Colors:** Light yellow, dark green, dark red, black
- **Intention:** "This cord protects this place in the north."
- **Charging cords:** Earth cord

East

- **Number:** Four for the square of protection
- **Colors:** Yellow, light blue, blue, white
- **Intention:** "This cord protects this place in the east."
- **Charging cords:** Air cord

South

- **Number:** Four for the square of protection
- **Colors:** Yellow, red, orange, white
- **Intention:** "This cord protects this place in the south."
- **Charging cords:** Fire cord

West

- **Number:** Four for the square of protection
- **Colors:** Blue, dark blue, dark green, dark purple
- **Intention:** "This cord protects this place in the west."
- **Charging cords:** Water cord

Handfasting

The ceremony of handfasting has become one of the most popular marriage rituals. Every wedding I have officiated has included a handfasting element. Tying two people's hands together makes a visual statement to the family and friends witnessing the marriage, and the feel of being bound to another person marks the moment of joining for the spouses.

You can twist a cord for use in handfasting. It's better to use a bulky yarn rather than embroidery thread and to ensure it is long enough to wrap around the hands; the result will be a nice flexible cord. If you choose to use a cord for a handfasting ritual, gift the couple with the cord. In addition, many couples make their own handfasting cord using a macramé technique that makes a thicker (and less flexible) cord.

> **Tip:** If you're officiating, practice wrapping the spouses' hands with the cord. Macramé cords are stiff and take a bit of work to get all the way around.

Charm
HANDFASTING CORD

- **Number:** Three, one for each spouse and another for the union
- **Colors:** Light red for love, dark green for prosperity, yellow for happiness
- **Intention:** "As these hands are tied, so these lives are tied together."

Commemorations

Cords make fun gifts to give to guests at celebrations such as weddings and birthdays. You can make the cords ahead of time or even teach the guests how to make them with each other. For this cord, pick the colors that make sense to you to match the occasion.

Friendship

You can make a cord to commemorate a friendship with one person or a group of people. Each person picks a color. Make the cord long enough so that it can be divided to give to each person. You divide the cord by making two knots and cutting between them.

A Final Note

The most important cord I ever made was for a coven mate who had cancer. It was a form of leukemia that came on fast and progressed quickly. He had a course of chemotherapy that made him very vulnerable to illness. There was a crisis moment during treatment when he would either recover or not.

The coven made a cord. We all made it in circle together and then gave him a piece of it. His piece was his end of the rope. The part we kept was our end of the rope. As the treatment progressed, we thought of him as going into the underworld and imagined ourselves plying out the rope as if lowering someone into a cave. At the crisis moment, we pulled with every ounce of magical strength we had to lift him back up into the land of the living.

He came out of chemotherapy and returned home. I hasten to add that he had really good medical care, a birth family who was praying for him, a wife and daughters who were working magic for him every day, and a wide set of friends who were all doing what they could to help. The cord was certainly not the only power the people who loved him used to get him back. It was the coven's focus though and it worked just as we wanted it to do.

For a while he was okay, then the cancer returned with a vengeance. In the meantime, he got to spend time with the coven, his wife, and his family and friends. He got to officiate at his daughter's wedding, a memory we all cherish. I vividly remember the hug he gave me at the last coven meeting we had with him. What would you give to have one more hug from your dear friend?

This book started and ended with stories about friends making cords together. In between, we've explored measuring a cord and using number and color and fiber in cord design, and we've planned lots of projects. Cords bring magic into every part of our lives. I hope that you are inspired to pick up some string and twist it!

Bibliography

Anderson, Geri. "Looms, weavers and the sacred snail on Mexico's Costa Chica." Mexconnect.com, April 3, 2011. http://www.mexconnect.com/articles/3755-looms-weavers-and-the-sacred-snail-on-mexico-s-costa-chica.

Anderson, Mali. "How to Make Natural Dyes from Fruits and Vegetables." Tom's of Maine. https://www.tomsofmaine.com/good-matters/thinking-sustainably/how-to-make-natural-dyes-from-fruits-and-vegetables.

Antico, Concetta. "Tetrachromancy." Concettaantico.com. https://concettaantico.com/tetrachromacy.

Austin, Pam. *Hand Spinning: Essential Technical and Creative Skills.* Ramsbury, UK: The Crowood Press, 2018.

Australia National Telescope Facility. "The Colour of Stars." https://www.atnf.csiro.au/outreach/education/senior/astrophysics/photometry_colour.htm.

Ayto, John. *Word Origins, The Hidden History of English Words from A to Z*. London: A&C Black, 2005.

Barber, Elizabeth Wayland. *Women's Work: The First 20,000 Years: Women, Cloth, and Society in Early Times*. London: W.W. Norton and Company, 1995.

Barber, E. J. W. *Prehistoric Textiles: The Development of Cloth in the Neolithic and Bronze Ages*. Princeton, NJ: Princeton University Press, 1991.

Barras, Colin. "World's oldest string found at French Neanderthal site." *New Scientist*, Sept. 13, 2013. https://www.newscientist .com/article/mg22029432-800-worlds-oldest-string-found-at -french-neanderthal-site/.

Bauer, Gerie. *Numerology for Beginners: Easy Guide to Love, Money & Destiny*. St. Paul, MN: Llewellyn Publications, 2000.

Beaumont, Peter. "Ancient shellfish used for purple dye vanishes from eastern Med." *The Guardian*, Dec. 5, 2016. https://www .theguardian.com/environment/2016/dec/05/ancient -shellfish-red-mouthed-rock-shell-purple-dye-vanishes -eastern-med.

Beckwith, Christopher I. *Empires of the Silk Road: A History of Central Eurasia from the Bronze Age to the Present*. Princeton, NJ: Princeton University Press, 2009.

Bentor, Yael. *Consecration of Images and Stupas in Indo-Tibetan Tantric Buddhism*. Leiden, NL: E.J. Brill, 1996.

Bertonis, Gloria. *Stone Age Divas, Their Mystery and Their Magic*. Bloomington, IN: Anchor House, 2011.

Bhatnagar, Satish C. *My Hindu Faith and Periscope, Volume 1*. Bloomington, IN: Trafford Publishing, 2012.

Bimbaum, Jennifer. "Consecration of Statues and Thangkas." *Snow Lion* newsletter, Winter 1995. https://www.shambhala.com/snowlion_articles/consecration-of-statues-and-thangkas/.

Black, Kate. "Clothing Textiles, From Fiber to Fabric: Acrylic." Utah State University Cooperative Extension. 2000. https://digitalcommons.usu.edu/extension_curall/1509/.

Bohr, Jakob, and Kasper Olson. "The Ancient Art of Laying Rope." Cornell University via arXiv.org, April 6, 2010. https://arxiv.org/abs/1004.0814.

Brooks, Lizzie. "Washing Instructions for Acrylic Yarn." eHow.com, August 31, 2017. https://www.ehow.com/how_7530669_washing-instructions-acrylic-yarn.html.

Brunello, Franco. *The Art of Dyeing in the History of Mankind.* Vicenza, Italy: Neri Pozza, Editore, 1973.

Buchanan, Rita. *A Weaver's Garden: Growing Plants for Natural Dyes and Fibers.* Loveland, CO: Interweave Press, 1987.

Buckland, Raymond. *Buckland's Complete Book of Witchcraft.* St. Paul, MN: Llewellyn, 2002. First published 1986.

Budge, E.A. Wallis. *Amulets and Superstitions.* New York: Dover Press, 1978. First published 1930 by Oxford University Press, H. Milford (London).

Cartwright, Mark. "Tyrian Purple." Ancient History Encyclopedia, July 21, 2016. https://www.ancient.eu/Tyrian_Purple/.

Cavanagh, Roy. "Sai Sin and the Sacred White Thread." Thaizer Thailand Travel Guide, June 5 2015. https://www.thaizer.com/buddhism/sai-sin-and-the-sacred-white-thread/.

Colour Blind Awareness. "Types of Colour Blindness." http:
    //www.colourblindawareness.org/colour-blindness/types-of-
    colour-blindness/.

Compassion in World Farming. "Welfare issues for sheep."
    https://www.ciwf.com/farm-animals/sheep/welfare-issues.

Cook, Michael. "Ahimsa (Peace) Silk, Why I Think it Doesn't Add
    Up." Wormspit.com. http://www.wormspit.com/peacesilk
    .htm.

Correa, Florencia Campos. *100 Pin Loom Squares*. New York: St.
    Martin's Press, 2015.

Crowley, Aleister. *777 and other Qabbalistic Writings of Aleister Crow-
    ley*. Edited by Israel Regardie. Boston: Weiser Books, 1977.

Daley, Jason. "Five Things to Know About the Recently Changed
    Migratory Bird Act." *Smithsonian* magazine, Dec. 27, 2017.
    https://www.smithsonianmag.com/smart-news/five-things
    -know-about-recently-changes-migratory-bird-act-180967646/.

Daniel, Frank Jack. "Jeans firms pollute Mexican city with blue
    dye." Reuters, May 2, 2007. https://www.reuters.com
    /article/us-mexico-jeans/jeans-firms-pollute-mexican
    -city-with-blue-dye-idUSN0233714020070503.

David, Alison Matthews. *Fashion Victims: The Dangers of Dress Past
    and Present*. London: Bloomsbury Visual Arts, 2015.

De Garis, Frederick, and Atsuharu Sakai. *We Japanese*. New York:
    Routledge and Kegan Paul, 2002.

De Mooij, Marieke. *Consumer Behavior and Culture: Consequences
    for Global Marketing and Advertising*. Los Angeles: Sage Publica-
    tions, 2011.

Deming, David. *Science and Technology in World History, Vol. 4: The
    Origin of Chemistry, the Principle of Progress, the Enlightenment*

and the Industrial Revolution. Jefferson, NC: McFarland and Company, 2016.

Donmoyer, Patrick J. *Powwowing in Pennsylvania: Braucherei and the Ritual of Everyday Life.* Kutztown, PA: Masthof Press and Pennsylvania German Cultural Center, Kutztown University, 2017.

Dudschus, Richard, and David Sledzinski. *Coloring the Classic Golden Dawn Tarot.* Renton, WA: D & S Publishing, 2005.

Duquette, Lon Milo. *Understanding Aleister Crowley's Thoth Tarot.* Woodbury, MN: Llewellyn Publications, 2017.

Elwell, Craig K. *Brief History of the Gold Standard in the United States.* Congressional Research Service, June 23, 2011. CRS Report for Congress, 2011.

Ewin, Elizabeth. *Fashion in Underwear: From Babylon to Bikini Briefs.* London: B.T. Batsford, Ltd., 1971.

Farrar, Janet, and Gavin Bone. *The Inner Mysteries: Progressive Witchcraft and Connection with the Divine,* second edition. Portland, OR: Acorn Guild Press, 2012. First published 2003 as *Progressive Witchcraft,* Career Press (Franklin Lakes, NJ).

Ferry, Tim. "Pasture degradation threatens Mongolia's cashmere industry." Nikkei Asian Review, September 7, 2017. https://asia.nikkei.com/magazine/20170907/Business/Pasture-degradation-threatens-Mongolia-s-cashmere-industry.

Gaboriaud-Kolar, Nicolas, Sangkil Nam, and Alexios-Leandros Skaltsounis. "A Colorful History, the Evolution of Indigoids," *Progress in the Chemistry of Organic Natural Products 99* (2014), A.D. Kinghorn, H. Falk, and J. Kobayashi, eds.

Geselowitz, Michael. "The Jacquard Loom: A Driver of the Industrial Revolution." The Institute, the IEEE News Source, July 18, 2016. http://theinstitute.ieee.org/tech-history/technology

-history / the-jacquard-loom-a-driver-of-the-industrial
-revolution.

Goodman, Brenda, MA. "Hot Flashes Linked to Lower Breast
Cancer Risk." WebMD, Jan. 28, 2011. http://www.webmd
.com/breast-cancer/news/20110127/hot-flashes-linked-to
-lower-breast-cancer-risk.

Greenpeace. "Toxic Threads: The Big Fashion Stitch-Up." Greenpeace International, 2012. http://www.greenpeace.org
/international/Global/international/publications/toxics
/Water%202012/ToxicThreads01.pdf.

Guiard, Patrice, PhD. *Planets, Colors and Metals.* 2004, http://cura
.free.fr/22plcome.html.

Handcock, Percy S. P. *Mesopotamian Archaeology: An Introduction to
the Archaeology of Mesopotamia and Assyria.* First published 1912
by Macmillan and Co (London). https://www.gutenberg.org
/files/45229/45229-h/45229-h.htm.

Hibi, Sadao, Kunio Fukuda, and John Bester. *The Colors of Japan.*
New York: Kodansha International, 2000.

Holm, Dan. "Why These Colors Don't Run: Dyeing the
Star-Spangled Banner." National Museum of American History, April 21, 2014. https://americanhistory.si.edu
/blog/2014/04/why-these-colors-dont-run-dyeing-the-star
-spangled-banner.html.

Holtzschue, Linda. *Understanding Color: An Introduction for Designers.* Hoboken, NJ: John Wiley and Sons, 2011.

How Products Are Made. "Rayon." http://www.madehow.com
/Volume-1/Rayon.html.

Hummel, John James, F.C.S. "The Dyeing of Textile Fabrics," *The New Technical Educator: An Encyclopaedia of Technical Education, Volume 4*. London: Cassell and Company Limited, 1898.

Humphrey, Nicholas. "The Colour Currency of Nature," Edited by Tom Porter and Byron Mikellides. *Colour for Architecture Today*, Studio-Vista (1976): 95–98.

Hurriyet Daily News. "Centuries-old fabric found in Catalhoyuk." February 3, 2014. https://www.hurriyetdailynews.com /centuries-old-fabric-found-in-catalhoyuk-61883.

Jorgensen, Susan S., and Susan S. Izard. *Knitting into the Mystery, A Guide to the Shawl-Knitting Ministry*. Harrisburg, PA: Morehouse Publishing, 2003.

Kabbalah Centre. "The Red String." Feb. 8, 2013. https://kabbalah.com/en/concepts/the-red-string.

Kan, Chi-wai. *A Novel Green Treatment for Textiles: Plasma Treatment as a Sustainable Technology*. London: CRC Press: 2015.

Kassinger, Ruth. *Dyes: From Sea Snails to Synthetics*. Brookfield, CT: Twenty-First Century Books, 2003.

Kastan, David, with Stephen Farthing. *On Color*. London: Yale University Press, 2018.

Klein, Herbert Arthur. *The Science of Measurement: A Historical Survey*. New York: Dover Publications, 1988.

Kluge, Charlie. *The Tallit*. Lake Mary, FL: Charisma House, 2016.

Kolev, Rumen. "Some Reflections about Babylonian Astrology." 2001. http://cura.free.fr/decem/09kolev.html.

Kvavadze, Eliso, Ofer Bar-Yosef, Anna Belfer-Cohen, Elisabetta Boaretto, Nino Jakeli, Zinovi Matskevich, and Tengiz Meshveliani. "30,000 Years old wild flax fibers—Testimony for fabricating prehistoric linen," *Science* 325 no. 5946 (2009): 1359. https://dash.harvard.edu/bitstream/handle/1/4270521 /BarYosef_PrehistoricLinen.pdf?sequence=2.

Lagan, Heather Alicia. *Chaldean Numerology for Beginners*. Woodbury, MN: Llewellyn Publications, 2011.

Larock, Vicki B. *Numerology: Divination & Numerology: Fortune Telling, Success in Career & Wealth, Love & Relationships, Health & Well Being*. (n.l.) Amazon Publishing, 2016.

Liddell, Henry George, and Robert Scott. "Pharmakon." *A Greek-English Lexicon*. Oxford, UK: Oxford University Press, 1843. http://www.perseus.tufts.edu/hopper/text?doc =Perseus%3Atext%3A1999.04.0057%3Aentry%3Dfa %2Frmakon.

Liles, J. N. *The Art and Craft of Natural Dyeing: Traditional Recipes for Modern Use*. Knoxville, TN: The University of Tennessee Press, 1990.

Loader, Rhea. *Dreamstones: Magic from the Living Earth*. London: Prism Press, 1991.

Lockshin, Prof. Rabbi Marty. "What Do Tzitzit Represent?" TheTorah.com. https://www.thetorah.com/article/what -do-tzitzit-represent.

Long, Priscilla. "How Mauve Was Her Garment," *The American Scholar*, June 19, 2013. https://theamericanscholar.org/how -mauve-was-her-garment/.

Los Angeles Police Museum. "LAPD's Finest, 140 Years of the World's Most-Storied Police Force," http://www.laphs.org /docs/blue-in-history-section.pdf.

Maanasvi, Dr. Manoj Kumar. *Principles of Pythagorean Numerology*. New Delhi: Educreation Publishing, 2018.

Mahamevnawa. "Receiving a blessing thread." Mahamevnawa.
com, April 7, 2018. https://mahamevnawabm.org/receiving
-a-blessing-thread-at-one-of-our-monasteries-in-sri-lanka/.

(no author) Martha Stewart. "Natural Dyes from Plants and Vegetables." MarthaStewart.com: https://www.marthastewart
.com/1518254/natural-dyes-from-vegetables-and-plants.

McCullough, D.G. "Deforestation for fashion: getting unsustain-
able fabrics out of the closet." *The Guardian*, April 25, 2014.
https://www.theguardian.com/sustainable-business/zara-h
-m-fashion-sustainable-forests-logging-fabric.

McLaughlin, Chris. *Hobby Farms: Rabbits: Small-Scale Rabbit Keeping*. Irvine, CA: Bow Tie Press, 2011.

Mead, Nathaniel M. "Benefits of sunlight: a bright spot for human
health," *Environmental Health Perspectives* 116, no. 4 (2008):
A160-7. doi:10.1289/ehp.116-a160. https://www.ncbi.nlm.nih
.gov/pmc/articles/PMC2290997/.

Mehta-Jones, Shilpa. *Life in Ancient Mesopotamia*. New York: Crab-
tree Books, 2005.

(no author) "Mental Health by the Numbers." National Alliance
on Mental Illness, NAMI.org. https://www.nami.org/learn
-more/mental-health-by-the-numbers.

Miller, Daniel, and Sophie Woodward, eds. *Global Denim*. Oxford:
Berg, 2011.

Mowry, Tamera. "The story behind our bracelets." Tam-
eramowry.com, June 15, 2015. http://www.tameramowry
.com/story-behind-bracelets/.

(no author) Mulberry Farms. Care & Raising Tips—FAQ. http:
//www.mulberryfarms.com/care-raising-tips-faq-12.html.

Munsell, Albert. "The Munsell Color Wheel Charts & Theory Behind Them." Munsell Color. https://munsell.com/color-blog/the-munsell-color-wheel-charts-theory-behind-them/.

(no author) National Institute of Mental Health (ND). "Statistics." National Institute of Mental Health. https://www.nimh.nih.gov/health/statistics/index.shtml.

Navran, Shakti Carola. *Jewelry and Gems for Self-Discovery: Choosing Gemstones That Delight the Eye and Strengthen the Soul.* St. Paul, MN: Llewellyn Publications, 2008.

Nichols, Wallace. *Blue Mind: The Surprising Science That Shows How Being Near, In, On, or Under Water Can Make You Happier, Healthier, More Connected, and Better at What You Do.* New York: Hachette Book Group, 2014.

Orr, Stephen. *The New American Herbal.* New York: Random House, 2014.

Ossola, Alexandra. "This Woman Sees 100 Times More Colors Than The Average Person." *Popular Science*, October 13, 2014. https://www.popsci.com/article/science/woman-sees-100-times-more-colors-average-person.

Parkes, Clara. *The Knitter's Book of Yarn.* New York: Random House, 2007.

Paspates, A. G. *The Great Palace of Constantinople.* Translated by B. D. William Metcalfe. London: Paisley, 1893.

Petit, Philippe. *Why Knot? How to Tie More than Sixty Ingenious, Useful, Beautiful, Lifesaving, and Secure Knots!* New York: Harry N. Abrams, 2013.

Pinch, Geraldine. *Magic in Ancient Egypt.* London: British Museum Press, 1994.

Purdy, Stephen R, DVM. "Review of the July 2017 Nunoa Project Veterinary Work in Peru August 2017." Nunoa Project, 2017. http://www.nunoaproject.org/Resources/July%202017 %20NP%20Summary%20web1.pdf.

Rabbi Ullman. "The Red String." Rabbiullman.com, June 19, 2004. http://wp.rabbiullman.com/the-red-string/.

Reimer, Miriam. "5 Food Companies That Serve You 'Wood.'" *The Street*, Mar. 2, 2011. https://www.thestreet.com/ story/11012915/1/cellulose-wood-pulp-never-tasted-so-good .html.

Reiner, Erica. "Astral Magic in Babylonia." *Transactions of the American Philosophical Society* 85, no. 4. Philadelphia: 1995.

Reis, João José, H. Sabrina Gledhill. *Death Is a Festival: Funeral Rites and Rebellion in Nineteenth-Century Brazil*. Chapel Hill, NC: University of North Carolina, 1991.

Replica Printing, "Why Do Printers Use CMYK?" October 24, 2016. https://replicaprinting.com/2016/10/24/why-do -printers-use-cmyk-instead-of-rgb/.

Riggs, Christina. *Unwrapping Ancient Egypt*. London: Bloomsbury Publishing, 2014.

Robinson, Rowan. *The Great Book of Hemp: The Complete Guide to the Environmental, Commercial, and Medicinal Uses of the World's Most Extraordinary Plant*. Rochester, VT: Park Street Press, 1995.

Sadtler, Samuel Philip, and Virgil Coblentz. *A Text-book of Chemistry: Intended for the Use of Pharmaceutical and Medical Students*. Philadelphia: J.B. Lippincott, 1906.

Schinzel, A. and H. Benger. "Water pollution by waste products of cellulose and rayon plants. II. Ground water pollution by waste water of the cellulose and rayon industries." *Arch Hyg Bakteriol*. June 1960, 144: 329–344. https://www.ncbi.nlm.nih.gov/pubmed/14442811.

Schmitz, Rob. "How Your Cashmere Sweater is Decimating Mongolia's Grasslands." National Public Radio, Morning Edition, Dec. 9, 2016. https://www.npr.org/sections/parallels/2016/12/09/504118819/how-your-cashmere-sweater-is-decimating-mongolias-grasslands.

Schoeser, Mary. *Silk*. New Haven, CT: Yale University Press, 2007.

Siegel, Ethan. "Why Does Earth Appear Blue from Space?" Forbes.com, March 4, 2016. https://www.forbes.com/sites/startswithabang/2016/03/04/why-does-earth-appear-blue-from-space/#7a37f3626bec.

Silverstein, Alvin, Virginia B. Silverstein, and Laura Silverstein Nunn. *Photosynthesis* (*Science Concepts* series). Minneapolis, MN: Twenty-First Century Books, 1998.

Skeat, Walter W. *The Concise Dictionary of English Etymology*. Hertfordshire, UK: Wordsworth Editions, 1993.

Soffer, Olga, James M. Adovasio, and David C. Hyland. "The 'Venus' Figurines, Textiles, Basketry, Gender, and Status in the Upper Paleolithic." *Current Anthropology* 41, no. 4 (August/October 2000): 511–537. https://doi.org/10.1086/317381.

Taussig, Michael. *What Color Is the Sacred?* Chicago: University of Chicago Press, 2009.

Taylor, Frederick. *Coventry*. London: Bloomsbury, 2017.

Teman, Elly. "The Red String: The Cultural History of a Jewish Folk Symbol." In *Jewishness: Expression, Identity, and Representation*, Simon J. Bronner, editor. Oxford: The Littman Library of Jewish Civilization, 2008.

(no author). "Thirsty for fashion? How organic cotton delivers in a water stressed world". Soil Association. https://www .soilassociation.org/media/19674/thirsty-for-fashion-soil -association-report.pdf.

Thompson, Daniel V. *The Materials and Techniques of Medieval Painting*. New York: Dover Publications, 1956.

Tierney, John, and Roy F. Baumeister. *The Power of Bad: How the Negativity Effect Rules Us and How We Can Rule It*. New York: Penguin Press, 2019.

Trachtenberg, Joshua. *Jewish Magic and Superstition: A Study in Folk Religion*. New York: Atheneum. Originally published 1939, Behrman's Jewish Book House, n.l.

Treadwell, Amy. *The Red Book of Luck*. San Francisco: Chronicle Books, 2018.

(no author) "Why does the ocean appear blue? Is it because it reflects the color of the sky?" *Scientific American*, October 21, 1999. https://www.scientificamerican.com/article/why-does -the-ocean-appear/.

Williams, Brandy. *White Light, Black Magic: Racism in Esoteric Thought*. Brandy Williams website, 2018. http:// brandywilliamsauthor.com/wp-content/uploads/2019/07 /White-Light-Black-Magic_-Racism-in-Esoteric-Thought.pdf.

Wingfield, Chris. "Witches' Ladder: the hidden history." http: //england.prm.ox.ac.uk/englishness-witchs-ladder.html.

Wipplinger, Michele. *Natural Dye Instruction Booklet: Everything You Need to Know About Dyeing and Painting with Natural Dye Extracts*. Boca Raton, FL: Earthues, 2000.

Woodford, Chris. "Nylon." Explain That Stuff!, January 31, 2019. https://www.explainthatstuff.com/nylon.html/.

Wright, Jennifer. "The History of Green Dye is a History of Death." Racked.com, March 17, 2017. https://www.racked.com/2017/3/17/14914840/green-dye-history-death.

Yamada, Haru, Orlando R. Kelm, and David A. Victor. *The 7 Keys to Communicating in Japan: An Intercultural Approach*. Washington, D.C.: Georgetown University Press, 2017.

Yamakage, Motohisa. *The Essence of Shinto: Japan's Spiritual Heart*. Translated by Mineko S. Gillespie, Gerald L. Gillespie, and Yoshitsugu Komuro. Tokyo: Kodansha International, 2006.

Index

C

R

S